MW00642122

Don't Wait Till
You're Dead

ALSO BY MATT FRASER

We Never Die

When Heaven Calls

The Secrets to Unlocking Your Psychic Ability

Don't Wait Till You're Dead

SPIRITS' ADVICE *from the* AFTERLIFE

MATT FRASER

G

GALLERY BOOKS

New York   London   Toronto   Sydney   New Delhi

Gallery Books
An Imprint of Simon & Schuster, LLC
1230 Avenue of the Americas
New York, NY 10020

First Gallery Books hardcover edition August 2024

GALLERY BOOKS and colophon are registered trademarks
of Simon & Schuster, LLC

Simon & Schuster: Celebrating 100 Years of Publishing in 2024

For information about special discounts for bulk purchases, please contact
Simon & Schuster Special Sales at 1-866-506-1949 or business@simonandschuster.com.

The Simon & Schuster Speakers Bureau can bring authors to your live event. For
more information or to book an event, contact the Simon & Schuster Speakers
Bureau at 1-866-248-3049 or visit our website at www.simonspeakers.com.

Interior design by Hope Herr-Cardillo

Manufactured in the United States of America

10 9 8 7 6 5 4 3 2 1

Library of Congress Control Number: 2024010220

ISBN 978-1-6680-2689-2
ISBN 978-1-6680-2691-5 (ebook)

This book is dedicated to my son, Royce.
Watching you grow up has opened my eyes to
a whole new meaning of life and love,
both in this world and the next.

CONTENTS

PREFACE

I remember like it was yesterday, getting the call from my publicist. *You did it, Matt! You made the* New York Times *Bestsellers list!*

I swear my heart stopped for a minute, tears came to my eyes, and I was overcome with gratitude for having been born with this incredible gift. I thought about all the people who had read my book *We Never Die: Secrets of the Afterlife*, and embraced my message. I wanted to call every one of them and thank them personally!

I began my career as a psychic medium to help and heal people, and it struck me that in addition to doing readings and hosting mediumship events, writing was one more way to reach out and transform lives.

Who would have thought a kid from Rhode Island could not only write a bestselling book, but change the way people feel about life and the afterlife!

It didn't take long for my excitement to shift into planning my next book—and I knew just what I wanted to write about. This book, *Don't Wait Till You're Dead*, is my thank-you gift to everyone who has helped me get here: my friends and family, my team, and everyone who has attended an event, followed me on social media, or purchased one of my books.

How is writing a book a thank-you gift? Before I answer, I'm going to ask you a question.

If you met a time traveler from the not-so-distant future who proved without the shadow of a doubt that he could help you predict the stock market or give you the winning lottery numbers, would you pay attention to what he had to tell you?

I'll bet you would shut off your phone and give him your undivided attention!

Well, I'm not that guy, and I can't help you win the lottery or grow your portfolio—at least not directly. But as a medium, I am able to reach across the veil between heaven and earth and learn from those who have made the transition to the afterlife and are in a position to look back upon their lives with perfect clarity.

Trust me, the insights they share are more valuable than winning the lottery!

Much of this wisdom comes the moment a soul transitions. There's something called a life review that everyone goes through when they get to heaven. I don't want to give away the whole book, but suffice it to say that when you die, you'll be surrounded by your guides, angels, and loved ones in heaven. Together you'll revisit your life in detail.

You'll see all of the wonderful moments, the people you loved, and the milestones you achieved. You'll also review the mistakes you made, the people you hurt, and the opportunities lost. When you're through, you'll finally understand what is truly important at the deepest, most profound level.

And that's where my gift to you comes in. I don't want you to wait until you die to have this "aha" moment. If you read this book from cover to cover and do the exercises in order to truly absorb "what Spirit wants you to know," you'll have the tools and understanding you need to live your very best life on earth—and die without regrets.

This is really important stuff, so I recommend taking the extra step and buying a notebook or journal to record your thoughts and observations as you read. You can also use it to record your answers and reactions to the exercises at the end of each chapter. Can you use your computer for this? Sure, but I have to tell you, there's something about picking up a pen and writing your answers that works to cement your intentions and solidify what you've learned.

One more thing, before we get started. As you make your way through these chapters, you'll see lots of references to your "spirit team" of angels, guides, and loved ones in heaven. Who are these celestial beings, and what roles do they play in your life? I'll explain that in more detail as we go, but let me give you a couple of key points now . . .

Your loved ones in heaven are connected to YOU, specifically. They may be the souls of friends or relatives you knew and loved, or they might be ancestors you never met, but who are deeply invested in you because of the blood bond you share. Your spirit guides were once mortal beings, but they never knew you in life. Their connection comes from their affinity to your situation, and their ability to help you on your path. They hold the "road map" to your destiny, and their job is to help you get there. You have one "main guide" and others who show up as needed throughout your life. Your guardian angels are the same—there's one main angel assigned to you (like Clarence in It's a Wonderful Life), but other angels might also appear at critical times. Unlike guides, angels never lived as mortals on earth. They are pure, celestial beings who protect you and look after your feelings and emotions. When I talk about your spirit team, that consists of all of these beings.

Sometimes I'll reference getting messages from "Spirit." As a medium, those messages are most often from loved ones in heaven, but guides and angels will also come through with messages and insights.

You don't have to wrap your head around all of this at once. All I ask is that you open your mind and your heart, and take this journey with me.

Thank you so much for being here. I'm delighted to be able to share what I've learned from the beautiful souls I connect with every day. Have a wonderful life!

Matt

Chapter 1

THE LIFE PREVIEW

This chapter starts at the very beginning. Actually that may not be entirely accurate. When you think of beginning your life's journey, the classic scene in the movies where a baby is being born may come to mind. We've all seen it dozens of times. Doctors and nurses in masks and scrubs gathered around the hospital bed. The father looking nervous and trying to help, and the mother giving it her all, every bit of her energy focused on pushing out that perfect, tiny, being. Suddenly the baby emerges, and everyone smiles when they hear the first amazing cry.

As I write these words, I can imagine the scene very vividly, but in the picture I have in my mind I know all the players personally. Alexa and I experienced the birth of our first child, Royce, this year, but like every newborn, Royce's existence actually began long before the beautiful wail that signaled that our precious new family member was healthy and strong. Actually, Alexa had the chance to get acquainted with Royce even before he was conceived, but more about that later!

WHAT EVERY MEDIUM KNOWS

When you're a medium, you're faced with the fact that life and death isn't an all-or-nothing proposition. I never thought of myself as a spiritual teacher, but because of my mediumship gift, I've had the opportunity to learn so much about life, heaven, and the afterlife. In addition to helping people heal from grief, I believe my purpose includes sharing that knowledge with the world.

During every reading, I not only receive messages from Spirit, but I learn something at the same time. Everything you read in this book is based on what I have heard and seen firsthand as a result of my ability to connect with souls in heaven. At that time, souls reveal who they are with, what they are doing, and share the lessons they have learned. Often, when the message comes through, it's as if a door opens and I get a little glimpse of the other side.

With that being said, I have learned that our souls are eternal, and there's a period of time where we come to this earth, live our physical existence, and fulfill our destiny. But there's infinitely more to "life" than that.

Which brings me to that age-old question . . .

WHAT IS THE MEANING OF LIFE?

When people ask that question, what they're really asking is, *What is the meaning of MY life, and why am I here?* At some point, everyone wonders what their purpose is on this earth. It can't just be to go through the mundane, day-to-day chores and responsibilities that we all endure, like working nine to five, cooking meals, doing dishes, and paying bills.

There must be more meaning and significance to our lives than that. Right?

Rest assured, your life has meaning, and I have good news. You don't have to find it alone. You're not the only one concerned about why you are here. Before you are born into the physical world, you have a team in heaven assigned to help you discover and achieve your true purpose, realize your potential, and even change the world in your own small (or large) way.

The best part is that this team isn't worried about themselves and their own success. They have no personal agenda. They've spent their time on earth, and their only purpose now is helping you make the most of your special gifts and talents.

Before we go on, and I lay out just who is on this team, stop and think about that for a minute and consider what an amazing thing it is to have a support group like this to guide you—a team that knows all the answers and has zero judgment or self-interest. Wow.

THE LIFE REVIEW
(A PREVIEW OF COMING ATTRACTIONS)

I don't want to give everything away in chapter one, but when I talk about the meaning of life, naturally, I think of the life review. It's all tied together. When you're alive, your spirit team helps guide you toward living your best life and fulfilling your destiny. Then, when you transition to heaven, you have a life review where you sit down with your team and review everything with perfect clarity. You see the impact you had on others, and the ramifications of the choices you made. But before you get there and receive those dazzling insights, you must take the first step . . . into life.

Packing Your Special Gifts

I said that we were going to start before the beginning, and we are. Your soul prepares for life in the same way you do when you are planning a trip. Before you get in the car or head to the airport, you think about what you need to bring and map out your itinerary. Preparation might begin well in advance of your trip.

When your soul gets ready to start its life journey, it works with its divine team to take an inventory of what to bring, which includes personality traits and special gifts. Of course, you'll learn lots of things throughout your life, but your innate talents and abilities, those things that make you uniquely you, are a God-given part of you. Athletes, artists, musicians, craftsmen, healers, leaders, people who have a special empathy for animals or people, and yes, psychics and mediums, have God-given gifts. They don't choose them, they're born with them.

We don't have total control of the life we're born into, but every one of us can use our gifts to leave the world a better place. Doing so doesn't happen by accident. Like many successful endeavors, life begins with a planning session—and this one takes place in heaven. That's the REAL beginning.

Charting Your Path

Before you're born, you gather with your team of spirit guides, angels, and family members in heaven. Your team shows you the people you'll be spending your time with on earth and reveals the divine road map that only souls in heaven have access to, a map that charts the entire course of your life.

This planning session allows your spirit team to educate you about what's ahead, and provides a preview of the key destiny points you will encounter.

What exactly is that "life planning session" like? First, let me say that I don't remember mine, and I don't know anyone who does. The insights I'm sharing come from souls I've connected with. That being said, this is how I see it.

Before you're born, it's like the scene in *The Lion King* where Simba's father, Mufasa, takes him up on the high rock and gives him a bird's-eye view of the kingdom. Like him, you see the people you'll be with, and where you'll live. Like Simba the lion cub, you survey the landscape with a more experienced soul at your side, and see your whole future laid out in front of you.

Getting the Lay of the Land

You can also picture your life planning session this way. Imagine you're moving to a new town, and have purchased your new home. You have a great Realtor who is showing you the area you'll live in, giving you the scoop on your neighbors, showing you the schools and shops. You're not going to know everything that will happen, but it's a nice orientation that makes you feel more comfortable with your move.

It's helpful to have that, because like moving into a new neighborhood, being born can be quite an adjustment. It's like graduating high school. Suddenly you're in the real world. Your divine existence is paused, and you're now launching yourself as a physical being. You have your gifts, your goals, and the road map you received in heaven, and it's up to you to live your life. Your team is still there to help. They're not in control of every move you make, but they all play important roles in helping you achieve your destiny.

I know I've just given you a lot of analogies! The reason is that what happens before you're born is something a lot of people have a hard time imagining. People always struggle with the idea that there's a destiny you are born with, while at the same time you also have free will. You might have a different opinion based upon your religious beliefs, but I'm trying to give you a clear picture based on what souls in heaven have shown and told me.

Getting to Know the Family Members
Who Passed Before You

Let's backtrack a bit. You are a soul in heaven ready to be born. It is at this time that you meet your spirit guide, angels, and those relatives who have passed on before you.

First, let's talk about the relatives. Some of those ancestors may have passed centuries earlier, but they're still part of your soul family. You might wonder what size group this is. Some people have a huge family tree, while others come from a smaller tribe. But because souls are eternal, chances are you have a very large soul group. Most people come for a reading and don't realize how many people are watching over them in spirit.

We might be born in this world but our soul starts its journey in heaven long before we arrive here in our physical form. Before we're born, we meet family members who have passed before us. We also meet and are assigned our spirit guide, angels, and special souls who will help us prepare for our journey, and walk with us through life on earth.

We get to spend a lot of time with our soul group before we're born. It's almost as if they're babysitting us before we start our journey. While the mother is pregnant, the soul of the baby is with its group in heaven.

I think it's comforting for people to understand that it doesn't matter if you're almost all alone on earth—you have a large network of souls who care about you in heaven. You will feel their presence throughout your life. Heaven and earth may seem very far apart, but we are really very closely connected. This reminds me of something that happened to Alexa before Royce was born.

I'LL SEE YOU IN MY DREAMS!

After we got married, Alexa and I knew we didn't want to wait too long to have a baby. We had such a positive feeling about it, and didn't anticipate any delay. We imagined that we'd try a couple of times, get pregnant, and have a baby. Turns out, it wasn't quite that easy. We were trying and trying, and nothing was happening. Every time Alexa took a pregnancy test and didn't see the pink line, she would get very distraught. One night she was in bed, crying. "What if I can't get pregnant?" she sobbed.

I was a little shaken up. Of course, I know that many people struggle with infertility, but I hadn't really considered that possibility for us. I told her everything would happen in time, but she didn't get any comfort out of that. I have to admit that for the first time, even though my psychic insights told me everything would be okay, I was starting to worry a little.

That night, Alexa cried herself to sleep, but to my surprise she woke up a new person.

She excitedly told me about a dream she had. "I dreamed I was pregnant and gave birth to a baby boy. We named him Royce. Matt, I've never had a dream like that—it felt so real!"

Alexa gave me all the wonderful details. She had spent so much time with our baby. She told me how tiny and perfect he was. She described in detail how he talked with his hands, loved Winnie-the-Pooh, and had a sassy personality. "He's just like me, Matt!" For weeks after the dream, she'd suddenly get quiet. She'd tell me, sadly, "I miss that little baby." She had met a baby in her dreams, but he was totally real to her. And he was real! Two weeks later we were thrilled to see a positive pregnancy test. A little later we found out it was a boy. Royce was born a little early and was very small. In fact, in every way, he was like he was Alexa's dream.

This story might sound unusual, but I wasn't surprised. When I was growing up, my mom, who is also a psychic medium, would have prophetic dreams about people and they often involved a pregnancy. I remember many mornings when Mom announced at breakfast that she had to call a friend or relative and tell them they would soon be welcoming a new arrival.

It turns out this happens a lot. Since sharing the story of Alexa's dream, I've had so many people reach out to me on social media and at events to tell me that they met their child in a dream before they were born. Just like we experienced, their dreams were detailed and accurate and felt more "real" than a normal dream.

Alexa is not psychic, and neither were many of these people, so how could this happen?

Here's what I believe . . .

Before we begin our lives on earth, and after we die, we spend time in heaven with our guides, angels, and family members. It's all one big circle and continuation.

Just like we don't remember being in the womb, we don't remember any of this until that day when we transition back home and suddenly recognize and remember all of these introductions and people.

WHY THAT BABY REMINDS YOU OF UNCLE WALTER

We are influenced by the time we spend with family members in heaven, even though we don't consciously realize it. That's why so many people display knowledge, personality traits, and mannerisms that surprise and confuse their family members. It may be hard to believe that the reason your son reminds you of someone who passed years before he was born is that he actually spent time with that person in heaven—but that's exactly what I'm telling you!

Maria's Story

My grandmother Mary passed before my sister Maria was born. My mother was devastated by the loss of her mom, and named my sister Maria to honor her. Then, when Maria was around four or five, my mom started to notice something. At first she didn't think much of it, but the evidence started to build up until she couldn't pass it off as coincidence! My sister displayed the exact same mannerisms, liked the same food, and had the same bold, bossy, opinionated personality as her grandmother. Even though my mother is a medium herself, and knows that this kind of thing happens, it still kind of freaked her out. She was so close to the situation that it made it hard for her to see what was happening, but eventually, she accepted the fact that my sister and her grandmother had spent time together in heaven.

MEET YOUR SOUL TEAM!

I've talked about the team that you meet in heaven that watches over you while you're on earth, but I want to make sure you understand a little more about the members of that team—your spirit guide, angels, and deceased loved ones.

Your Spirit Guides Lead You Through Life

A spirit guide is a soul that once lived here on earth that is now in heaven. They are not related to you and have no ancestral connection to your family. So why are they your guide? They choose you based on their ability to help you.

Your spirit guides know all about you. In fact, they possess a "road map" to your entire life. They know the challenges you are going to face, the people who will be important in your life, the special gifts you will be born with, and the important milestones you are destined to encounter. They know everything that is predetermined about your journey to this world. That doesn't mean they can anticipate or control your every move or that your every move is predetermined. You still have free will. But they do know where you are meant to go, and can anticipate many of the destiny points along the way.

Although people might have a few spirit guides around them, you have one main spirit guide that acts commander in chief! This is known as your "main guide."

How do you get matched up with your guide? They are not relatives or ancestors, so there's no genetic link. Instead, your guide sees something in you that reminds them of themselves. They know they are in a unique position to help you, and helping you is satisfying to them. It's like in the *Harry Potter* books, where the wand chooses the student.

Think of all the people who have died over thousands and thousands of years. There are so many possible guides, but there is only one main guide assigned to you, and you have a very special connection.

This guide once lived life and experienced similar struggles and challenges to what you are going through. They can't change their past, but they can help themselves by guiding you to avoid the mistakes they made.

If your guide was once a doctor, they might choose a soul who is destined to go into the same type of work so that they can guide them. They know your life like it's a book, or a movie, before it happens. They know your personality, your dreams, and your ambitions.

Helping You Through Life by Guiding,
Not Controlling

Your guide is like a GPS for your soul. They do their very best to nudge you and keep you on course. It's not easy, because you have a mind of your own. It's just like when you're taking a long trip. You know where you want to go, and you put the destination into your navigation system in your car or phone. But how many times do you not listen to the GPS? You might decide to take a toll road, or not, regardless of what your navigation system suggests. You might want to get off the freeway to avoid traffic, or you might need to stop for a cup of coffee and a donut. When I drive, my GPS is constantly rerouting (I have a hard time passing up Dunkin' Donuts), but no matter how often I detour, it will always get me to the destination. Living life is like driving a car. You can only see the road ahead of you. But your navigation system sees the big picture.

Roles of a Spirit Guide

To better understand your whole team, it will help if you know what each member is responsible for.

Your spirit guide helps you chart your course and make your plan. As you go through your life, they will do everything they can to keep you on your path.

Some of their responsibilities include:

› Preparing you for the journey ahead

› Supporting you in fulfilling your life's purpose

› Helping you to discover your gifts and abilities

› Introducing you to your soul mate

› Putting you in contact with influential people, both friends and adversaries, who will participate in your life journey

› Exposing you to lessons that help you to evolve and grow

› Signaling you when you're drifting off course, or rerouting you so you wind up where you are meant to

Your spirit guide is a very helpful being to have in your corner, but there is a catch. They are big-picture focused. They are not concerned with your day-to-day emotional well-being, just like your GPS doesn't care if you're hungry and need to stop for a bathroom break. Their goal is to help you navigate as many life lessons, challenges, and opportunities and prepare you for what's to come in the future. They care about you, but they understand that some of the greatest challenges can teach you the most important lessons, even if they might cause emotional distress in the moment.

Some of the most difficult situations can make the biggest difference in your life. When you're going through a divorce, you might wonder why this is happening. It may feel like the pain and loss are too much to bear, but when you look back years later, you understand how that challenge shaped you and helped you to transform into the person you were meant to be. Take me, for example . . .

Hard Times in High School Prepared Me
to Become a Successful Medium

When I was in high school, I wasn't like the other kids, and I was bullied every day. That experience was horrible, but looking back, there was some value in that pain. First of all, it made me tough, resilient, and determined. Those are important traits for a public figure who is regularly onstage, on radio, and on television. Being a medium makes it even harder, because for every fan there is another person who doubts what I do. I have no problem dealing with negative press, skeptics, or trolls who call me a fraud, make fun of how I dress, or post hurtful messages. After years of being bullied when I was younger, when I encounter negativity I can now say, "Bring it on!"

I know that I would have a hard time living life in the public eye if I hadn't gone through such severe bullying when I was younger. I almost wish I could thank those kids who teased and tortured me, because I would not be the medium—or the person—I am today without having gone through that experience. I know that it was my guide who kept me on course and gave me the strength to go on. There was a time when I hid my true self because I wanted to avoid being bullied. I would have opted out of pain back then if I had the chance. But instead I continued on my winding journey through high school, and EMT training, to find myself here. Every day, I'm grateful to my guide for leading me to this life, where I can help and heal people every day.

TRANSFORMING HARDSHIP INTO HEALING

I remember years ago I did a reading for a woman whose parents had been addicts. Sadly they were never able to get clean, and their addiction ended up killing them. My client had struggled with her own addictions when she was young, and was going down a destructive path too, until their death caused her to change course. Now she is a sponsor and advocate for at-risk youth—and is very effective at helping them because of her own experience. In the reading, her mother came through and commended her daughter for staying clean and doing what she herself had been unable to do. Her mother confirmed that the woman's spirit guide is leading her to people she can help, and THEIR guides in turn are leading them to her to be helped. The guides team up and work together for the mutual benefit of the people they are helping.

Everyone Needs a Guardian Angel

Your spirit guide chooses you based on your shared destiny points, but your guardian angel is assigned to you by the higher powers of heaven. We all have a few angels that watch over us, but there's a single angel who is our "official" guardian angel. Life can be hard, and your guardian angel is there to help and support you through the emotional issues that arise during your time on earth.

Your guardian angel will be there to help you navigate:

› Loss and disappointment

› Depression and anxiety

› Breakups

› Illnesses and health scares

› The deaths of people you care about

Guardian angels are like loving, empathetic relatives who know you better than you know yourself, and can see your whole life in perspective. They want only what's best for you, and will wrap you in their protective wings when things get tough. That might sound a lot like a spirit guide, but there's one key difference. Your spirit guide's job is to help you navigate your life's course, leading you through experiences, introducing you to people you need to meet, and taking you to the places you need to go. They're not overly concerned with your your feelings and emotions. That's where angels comes in! While you're on your journey, angels are there to provide emotional support and protection—and hold your hand through the whole experience.

Like your spirit guides, you have one "main angel," but there are other angels that are part of your team, and are available to help as needed.

Your angel will:

› Warn you of impending danger.

› Uplift you emotionally.

› Encourage and cheer you on when you're making tough decisions.

› Remind you that there's good in life and encourage you during the dark times.

› Surround you with love and give you strength when you need it the most.

› Heal your mind, body, and spirit.

› Remind you of the good you've done and encourage you to fulfill your potential.

› Send you signs and messages.

› Give you courage and help you manifest your dreams.

Who Is Your Guardian Angel?

People always ask me if someone who has passed on, such as a grandmother or family member, is their "guardian angel," and although they are like an angel, and do watch over you, guardian angels are completely different.

Angels are supreme celestial beings that are like the guidance counselors of heaven. Pretty cool, right? I'll bet you never knew you had your own divine counselor up above.

Angels are problem solvers, peacemakers, and most of all, emotional healers when times are tough. You might be thinking, *How can they know and help so many people and do such amazing things?* Your guardian angel is an all-loving, divine being who wants to see you happy and enjoying life. Before you are even born into this world, your guardian angel is assigned to watch over you and to care for you. They have spent centuries learning about you so they can do the best job possible of protecting, supporting, and healing you. You are introduced to them as a baby when you are in heaven, and you reunite and meet them again when your journey in the physical world comes to a close.

Although your guardian angel is meant to help and protect you, they can only be of service if you listen to the messages they send to you. As human beings, we have been given free will, and no guardian angel can overstep this. Know that when you are doing something dangerous or self-destructive, your guardian angel is trying everything possible to stop it, but they cannot overstep the boundaries of free will.

Bottom line, it's your life, and the time you spend here on earth is where you make all of your life choices and learn your greatest lessons before returning home. Part of your guardian angel's job is recording the life decisions that you make, and your life events, so when you make your transition to the other side you will be able to clearly see all of the lessons you learned. Your life review will allow you to see the whole of your life in perspective, and everything will suddenly make sense.

Connecting With Your Guardian Angel

You are the most important person in the world to your guardian angel. They want you to walk through life knowing that you have a special friend who believes in you and is always by your side. If you have not felt the presence of your guardian angel with you, it's easy to connect with them. One way is to start each morning by waking up and simply saying hello to them. By speaking with your angel, you open a conversation in which they can respond back to you. Your angel wants to be able to speak to you but can only do so when you are ready to open your mind. Engaging in a conversation will help you feel closer to them. It's amazing what happens when you invite them into your life. They will be with you no matter what, but being aware of them is comforting, and helps them do their job in the best way possible.

A Soul Gets a Second Chance at Life

I did a reading once for a woman who had lost a baby very early in her pregnancy. Shortly after her miscarriage, her father passed. This loss was devastating to her, because the two were so close, and he had been hanging on to life, hoping she would get pregnant again so he could meet his grandchild. Unfortunately he died before this could happen, but it wasn't long after that she found out she was pregnant again. During our reading, her dad came through and told us something that surprised us both. He had met his grandson in heaven, and he let her know that the soul of this baby she had lost was getting a second chance in the body of the new baby. He assured his daughter that her second pregnancy would result in a healthy baby. The woman was so happy to hear this, and especially loved knowing that her father had met his grandchild after all.

Does this happen every time a woman miscarries? It doesn't, but sometimes, when the pregnancy ends very early, the soul gets another chance.

ANGELS, GUIDES, AND LOVED ONES
IN HEAVEN

People often ask me if their loved ones, like the father in the story I just shared, will be their guardian angels. It's important to remember that angels are divine beings who have never lived in the physical world, but family members who have passed over are part of the spirit team (along with angels and guides) that will continue to support them as they live their lives, and will sometimes act like guardian angels without taking the official role.

As souls make the transition into the real world, they remain connected to the divine through their spirit team and their intuition. Just like with any mentor, teacher, or caretaker, that relationship will evolve over time.

Rounding Out the Team:
Family Members Who Have Passed

You are assigned your spirit guide and guardian angel before you were born, but the souls of family members are also with you. Some of them may have passed many years earlier, but they can actually become part of your soul team at any time. People often feel the presence of their mother, father, or grandparent after they pass. This is not denial or wishful thinking. You can take comfort in the fact that when you lose someone in this world they join you on your journey from the other side. Your soul team keeps growing, and although you might not have that person around in the physical sense, they are very much with you.

A Winning Team Works Together

Your spirit guide and angels must work together to support you on your life's journey. They also connect with the spirit guides and angels of others when your paths are meant to cross. For example, if you are at a point in your life where you are ready to meet your soul mate, the guides of both individuals will coordinate events to bring you together. Your angels will give you the emotional support and courage you need to make that special connection.

Every member of your "team" has something in common—YOU! They all want what's best for you. Their mission is to help you live your best life and avoid pitfalls and setbacks. Like we talked about, they cover different territory. The angel is there to protect and encourage you emotionally, while your guide is there to keep you on course to fulfill your ultimate goals. Your relatives in heaven are part of the team to send love and lend support in all kinds of ways.

SPIRITUAL PRACTICE

HOMEWORK FROM HEAVEN

At the very, very beginning, your destiny was mapped out and the universe determined the answers to these questions. Now it's time for you to rediscover these answers.

Remember when I told you to get the most out of this book by using a notebook or journal to record your thoughts and observations? Well, now's that time, so grab a pen and let's get started with some questions!

› What are your gifts, what is your destiny, and how will you change the world?

› What did you love as a child?

› Do you have a hidden talent or ability that you haven't shared with anyone?

› How are you unlike anyone else? What makes you unique and special?

Answering these questions helps you find your life's purpose and the gifts and skills you were born with. Don't second-guess yourself; let your intuition guide you. Open yourself up to divine guidance by asking your guides and angels to drop ideas into your mind.

A MESSAGE FROM YOUR SOUL TEAM

When you are feeling sad or defeated or are at a crossroad in your life, close your eyes and let us lead you. Remember that we, your angels, loved ones, and spirit guide, can help you to see the road ahead clearly. Remind yourself that we believe in you even when you do not believe fully in yourself. Take a deep breath and trust in the process. Keep in mind that you are not meant to see your whole journey before it happens. When it comes to your story, it's not possible to skip to the ending. You have to let your life unfold like a book, page by page. You have us by your side to guide and protect you. We have your back. What is important is that you don't lose faith.

Remember that you can talk to us at any time and we are here to listen to you.

Chapter 2

THE SOUL'S ARRIVAL ON EARTH

In chapter 1, I provided you a glimpse into what happens at the very beginning of the soul's earthly journey. This is the planning phase, where the soul gathers with a team that consists of their guides, angels, and family members who have passed over, to chart the course of your life.

It doesn't feel entirely accurate to use the word *beginning* in this context, since souls are eternal and their journey is a circle that begins and ends at the same place—heaven. As humans, having a beginning, middle, and end makes it easier for our minds to grasp this concept, but try not to take that time line too literally.

Within that circle, there are two major transition points: the first when the soul enters the physical world, and the second when the physical body dies and the soul crosses back over.

At what point between conception and birth does the soul actually enter the body? I don't have a clear answer to that. It's different for each soul, but suffice it to say that the physical stage of the soul's journey starts at that time. Those two transitions feel a bit different, both to the soul itself and the people around it.

TRANSITIONING INTO THE PHYSICAL WORLD

When you die, the shift can feel very sudden. One minute you're here, and the next thing you know, you're in heaven. It's not jarring or traumatic—no matter how you die, the actual crossing over is very peaceful—but it's instant, as if someone flicked a switch.

When a baby is born, it's not like that. Instead of happening all at once, the soul's transition feels more gradual. Babies have one tiny foot in each world for a while. They've been spending time in heaven connecting with their soul team and charting their life's course, and when they're born, they are still very close to that divine space, and their team.

A Perfect Beginning

Have you ever noticed how newborns seem so pure and angelic, especially in the first few weeks of life? I had heard new parents talk about that, but I didn't experience it firsthand until my son, Royce, was born. As a medium, I'm sensitive to energy, and Royce radiated the most pure, divine energy I'd ever experienced in a living person. That energy is still there (he'll always be a little angel to me), but as he settles in and becomes more aware of his physical surroundings, it's shifting. I believe that when babies arrive, they exist for a while in the center of two overlapping realms, a sacred space that's a combination of heaven and earth.

The Soul's Transition

My connection with souls on the other side has given me an understanding of the journey. We start out as celestial beings, free of pain, hurt, jealousy, and fear. That begins to change when we enter our earthly bodies. We come into the earth as pure love, and gradually we pick up the behaviors that allow us to exist in this world. It would be nice to live a heavenly life on earth, but that's not why we're here. Our purpose is to fulfill our destiny and learn lessons that help our soul to grow. Then when we pass, it's as if we go through a screen that filters out the earthly qualities, and we become pure divine energy again.

Heavenly Visitations

The same way family and friends gather from near and far to see a newborn baby, spirits do the same. Because we spend time with our loved ones before we are born they continue to check up on us when we transition to this world.

That is why some babies will stare at, interact with, or laugh at things that are not there. Chances are if this is happening they are seeing the spirit world. You might pick up on this as well. For example, I had a woman on Facebook send me a video of orbs circling around her baby's crib. She had no idea what was happening and was alarmed. When I looked at the video I could see the orbs were the souls of her loved ones paying a visit to her little one.

BIRTHDAYS AND HOLIDAYS ARE
ALWAYS A TIME TO GATHER

Our guides and angels visit us as babies, and as we grow they appear to us less and less. It's like your extended family who want to be there for every milestone in the first few months. They might find reasons to drop in every day to help the new parents and shower the child with love and attention, but that doesn't last forever.

When Royce was born, there were days when Alexa and I were exhausted and just wanted our house to ourselves, but there was so much love from so many friends and family members that we couldn't turn anyone away. Like with any baby, the visits slowed down after a while. The stream of guests subsided, and I'm pretty sure most people outside our immediate family will soon be content with sharing special occasions like birthdays and holidays.

In fact, the joyful energy generated by special occasions attracts heavenly guests as well as living relatives. Nothing brings members of your spirit team closer, especially your loved ones who have passed, than seeing friends and family gathered together to celebrate a birthday, anniversary, or holiday. The warmth and love attracts them like a magnet, so if you find yourself thinking, *I wish Grandma was here*, you can take comfort in the fact that she most likely is!

WHEN THE PROTECTIVE BUBBLE
STARTS TO DISSIPATE

When a baby is born, they don't know anxiety or fear, but that changes sooner than you would think. Royce started out happy to be held by anyone, but a nurse let us know that for most infants, that doesn't last. At a few months of age, she said, Royce would experience an awareness of strangers and start to show some fear and anxiety when left alone. Royce is still a trusting baby, and he's used to having a lot of people around, but Alexa and I are noticing small signs of the separation anxiety the nurse warned us about. He definitely knows who his parents are, and it's kind of cute to see him tracking Alexa and me with his eyes when someone else is holding him, almost like he's watching a tennis match.

It's as if a baby is born in a protective bubble surrounded by their spirit team, and as time goes on, they have to prepare themselves to live in this world. That's when the circles I talked about earlier, the ones that intersect when the baby is born, start to separate.

WHEN AN IMAGINARY PLAYMATE IS SOMETHING MORE

I did a reading for a family recently. I didn't know that the mother had lost several babies due to miscarriage until the grandmother came through and showed me that she was in heaven with the souls of all those tiny babies. That was just the first surprise in what turned out to be an extraordinary reading. Grandma stepped back, and a little girl came through who had been a twin. Her sister had lived and was there for the reading, but the more fragile twin sister only survived for a short time after birth. Her soul came through with such amazing memories of her brief life, especially the love that her parents had for her. Her mother was so happy to know that this precious little being had known how much she was loved, but here's the crazy part! Like many children, the sister who survived had an imaginary friend, and that friend was actually the twin who had passed over. She confirmed that her imaginary friend's name was the name that her parents had given her twin sister. She wasn't a guide or angel, but a member of her soul team. It was beautiful for both of them, because even though her sister wasn't there physically, she got to experience life through her surviving twin. Everyone in the room was shocked when I asked if the twin (who was now grown-up) had a butterfly tattoo—because she and her parents had just gotten tattoos to honor the twin who had passed over years earlier. She pulled down the shoulder of her T-shirt to show me, and everyone got chills!

Imaginary friends are not always visitors from heaven, but as a medium, I often hear about siblings and other souls who become "imaginary friends" to young children. It's a beautiful thing when a child is able to have that kind of connection with a loving soul. As parents, it's good to keep an open mind, and listen without judgment when your child tells you about a friend that only they can see.

WHO DROPPED THE COLOGNE?

I think you'll like this story, and even though it happened to me, I don't think it's because I'm a medium! I'm 100 percent sure the same thing could happen to anyone, so take this as a reminder to keep your eyes, ears, and NOSE open for signs from heaven. Here goes . . .

My grandfather wanted nothing more than to stay alive to see me get married and to be there when our first child was born. I'm glad that he lived long enough to get to know Alexa, who he absolutely adored, but he passed away before he was able to attend our wedding or to meet the baby.

Naturally, from the moment Royce was born, I was expecting him to send some kind of validation that he was with us, but nothing happened for a while.

When my grandfather was alive, he always loved to dress up, which included splashing on some nice cologne. When I was a teenager, I worked at Abercrombie & Fitch, and my grandfather became obsessed with the Fierce cologne that we sold. Every so often I would surprise him with a bottle and it became his signature smell. He loved it so much that when he passed away, I sprayed his casket with Fierce and left one last bottle with him.

Fast-forward to about six weeks after Royce was born, when I had an experience I would never forget. I woke up early in the morning and picked Royce up out of his bassinet. I brought him into the nursery to change his diaper and feed him, then I laid him down in his crib and went to the kitchen to warm up a bottle. When I returned to his room with the warm bottle, I was taken aback by the smell of Fierce permeating the room. There was no doubt in my mind that my grandfather was there, checking on Royce.

I immediately yelled, "Alexa, come quick!" I had to find out if she could smell it too. She walked into the room and the first thing she said was, "Did you drop a bottle of cologne?" I laughed and told her that Poppy was here. She immediately got the chills, and knew I was right. It meant the world to both of us to know that he was able to meet his grandson.

It's not unusual to feel loved ones in heaven around your young children. Even if they died before the child was born, they will show up to check up on them from time to time. It happens a lot when the child is young, because their Spirit connection is still so strong, but those loving souls will still be there for the child as they grow up and get older.

WHEN YOUR HEAVENLY VISITOR
SKIPS A GENERATION

While we're on the subject, I want to remind you that it's important to keep an open mind and accept that souls in heaven know what's best for you and your family. It's not always easy. Imagine you lose your mom or dad, and, more than anything in the world, you're longing for a sign that they are still with you. Nothing comes, until suddenly your child starts talking about Grandma or Grandpa! They might say that Grandma visited them at night, or point to a picture and say, "Grandpa played with me yesterday." You're happy that they had the connection, but you might wonder why your parents aren't visiting YOU. *What am I, chopped liver?* you ask yourself. No, you're not. There are all kinds of reasons why this can happen. It might be that you are busy and not as open to noticing their presence or picking up on the signs they send. But it might be deeper than that.

That was the case when my grandmother passed. My mother wanted a sign from her so bad, but Grandma would only come to me. We had been so close when I was young, so I was thrilled that after she died she would visit me at night and play with me. My mother couldn't figure out why she wasn't coming through to her, so I finally asked my grandma. She let me know that my mother was in such deep mourning that she was afraid to contact her. She felt that my mom needed to move on with her life. Because of that, my grandmother limited her visits to me. In that way, she could still be around the family she loved and still allow my mother to stay focused on her husband, her children, and living her best life.

Trust that souls in heaven are coming from a place of love, and will do what's in your best interest. They might not give you what you ask for in exactly the way you expect, but they know what's right for you. If you wanted a sign from your mother and never got one, and now she is there for your child, don't be upset. The fact that you can sense through your child means she is there for you, too. A baby or child provides a gateway where that soul can connect with both of you.

MOM WAS NEVER THAT WAY WITH ME!"

This is something every medium can relate to. People can change so much when they pass over that you might not recognize them when they come through in a reading. You may have had a mom who was detached and not present, or a dad who was always working.

Suddenly they come through in a reading and they're showing so much love for you and your children. *What's going on?* you ask yourself. *They were never like this when they were alive.*

The explanation is pretty simple. People go through lots of changes both during their lives, and after they pass.

WHO ARE THESE PEOPLE?

Growing up, I had nice, normal parents. They had busy lives, they nagged me about homework, and they expected me to do chores. Fast-forward to today, and as I watch them sitting on the floor playing with Royce, I have to ask myself, *Who are these people?* They're super-nurturing grandparents, and are constantly showering him with attention and affection. I know it's not that they love him more than they loved me, but they're in a different place in their lives, and any parent will tell you that grandchildren are different.

It's the same when a soul passes over. Throughout their time on earth, they might have been struggling with all kinds of things, but when they get to heaven, they leave their baggage behind. Whatever was holding them back from being there for you in life is gone, and they are in a space of pure love.

When you think about it from that perspective, it won't be so surprising when your loved ones start sending your signs from heaven, or come through with loving messages in a reading. They might also try to make up for lost time by coming through to their grandchildren. If you feel that happening, know that it's their way of feeling close to YOU, as well as watching over your children. If your relationship with your parents wasn't what you needed, allow this new connection to open the door to healing.

Because babies are so strongly connected to Spirit, they're likely to receive visits from loved ones on the other side. But since they can't talk, it can be hard to know if this is happening. Even children who can talk have a hard time understanding what's happening, and an even harder time communicating their experience to you.

HOW CAN YOU KNOW IF YOUR BABY OR CHILD IS RECEIVING VISITS FROM HEAVEN?

› You see your baby smiling or gesturing at something that is not there.

› You start consistently noticing orbs and distortions in photos.

› Your child references someone who passed before they were born.

› They mention something that they couldn't possibly know—like a significant event or a hobby relating to the deceased.

› Your child talks about an imaginary friend.

› Your child is frightened by something that is not there.

› Your child starts telling you they "see ghosts."

HELPING YOUR CHILD UNDERSTAND THEIR SPIRIT CONNECTION

If you sense this is happening to your child, or they share one of these experiences, what do you do? You don't want to scare them, so try to demystify the encounter. Be very calm and matter-of-fact. Listen to what your child tells you. Don't make a big deal out of it. It's best to make the loved ones in heaven a part of their everyday life. Have pictures of them around, and tell stories about the time you spent together. My mother would tell me that my loved ones were always with me. Sometimes she would point up to the sky and tell me, "Grandma is there and she's looking down on you!"

Talk to your child in terms they can understand. For example, my dad was in the military and he wasn't around all the time. As a little boy, I was confused about why he didn't come home to dinner every night like my friends' fathers did, but my mom did the best she could to make me feel close to him. Every time a plane passed by she'd tell me to wave to Daddy. It's the same way with loved ones in heaven.

It's important to help your child feel connected and comfortable with loved ones who have passed, and give them the tools to relate to these heavenly visitors. Here are some ways to get the conversation started.

› Keep the conversation simple and loving. Talk about their invisible phone line where they can talk to Grandma, or come up with a familiar way to describe it that is unthreatening and makes sense.

› Bring up family members who have passed in a calm, cheerful way, especially when your child asks about people in pictures. If it seems appropriate, let them keep a photo in their room.

› Be open and welcoming. When they talk about an imaginary friend, don't joke around about it with other people, or make a big deal out of it. Take your cues from your child when it comes to involving the friend in family activities.

YOU WERE BORN PSYCHIC, AND YOUR INTUITION IS STILL PART OF YOU

We're focusing on babies and children in this chapter, but don't forget that as an adult, you can still have that connection. Infants and children are born with an innate psychic connection that allows them to easily see and hear the departed. As an adult, you might not consider yourself psychic, and you may have forgotten all about the Spirit connection you had as a child. Your natural intuition never leaves you, but you might not be conscious of what it is telling you, or you may hear that inner voice, but choose to ignore it.

Keeping the Connection Alive

Some people (older children as well as adults) never lose their connection to heaven. Their intuition remains strong throughout their lives. At the time when many children naturally start to become less imaginative and more focused on fitting in with the kids at school, these psychic, highly sensitive, and empathetic children stand out. They have psychic insights, pick up on emotions and clues, and are much more aware of the souls and angels around them.

Intuition—the Voice of Your Soul Team

We all carry a direct phone line to heaven, and it is called intuition. Your intuition is that gut feeling that speaks to you from deep within. But where is that voice really coming from? True intuition comes from your soul, and the angels, guides, and loved ones who are connected to you at that level. Bottom line, intuition is how your spirit team speaks to you. Trust me, they know what they're talking about, and the more aware and accepting you are of this, the better you can benefit from their help and guidance.

I feel very connected to my grandparents, and several other people who have passed over. I also am very tuned in to my guides and angels. I talk to them all the time! But everyone doesn't have the same desire to hear from their spirit team, and that's perfectly fine.

In the same way you decide how connected you are to your family members, you get to decide how connected you will be with your spirit team. Some people are very influenced by their families and others are totally estranged. Most are somewhere in between. Families are a little different, because you're dealing with human beings with flaws. There might be a good reason to keep some family members at arm's length. Your spirit team is always coming from the best place, having your best interest at heart, but you can still decide how much interaction you want to have with them.

Your connection with Spirit can be developed and enhanced. The more mindful and open you are to your intuition, the more connected you will be to your guides, angels, and loved ones in heaven. They may make their presence known to you differently than they did when you were a child, because they usually don't want to scare you by appearing as a ghost. Instead, they send you signs.

————— TIMES WHEN YOU FEEL YOUR INTUITION AT WORK: —————

> You get a sense that something isn't right with a person, place, or situation.

> You're drawn to something or someone and you don't know why.

> You hear an inner voice speaking to you.

> You have vivid dreams that feel important or different.

> You have an "aha moment" or breakthrough out of the blue.

› You sense a red flag when dealing with a person.

› You sense danger in a situation.

› You have a close call and feel as if someone or something "saved you."

› You sense something about another person based on their energy.

› You are very sensitive and feel other people's emotions.

What Happens When You Ignore Your Intuition?

As adults, we sometimes discount our intuition because it goes against our rational thought system. We ignore our gut, and allow ourselves to be swayed by what we want to believe is true, or by the opinions of others.

For example, you might be very attracted to someone, and your spirit guide is trying to warn you that they're not for you by throwing up all kinds of red flags. But you don't want to hear that! When it comes to re-lationships, a combination of infatuation and wishful thinking will often cause you to discount what your guides are telling you. You have free will, and always have the option to ignore your intuition. But remember, your intuition is never wrong, and if you choose to override it, you might find yourself in the wrong place, or with the wrong person, wishing you could rewind and start over.

Remember that your intuition is a voice inside you that develops over time, and gets stronger and more accurate the more you listen to it.

SPIRITUAL PRACTICE

JOURNALING PROMPT—HOW TO FEEL MORE CONNECTED TO YOUR INTUITION AND YOUR SOUL TEAM

You have access to all the wisdom in the universe, if you open yourself up to your connection with your guides, angels, and loved ones in heaven.

Meditate on these questions, and then, without editing yourself, use your journal and write down your insights:

> › Think about the two sides of you, your spiritual side and the earthly practical side. Are they in balance?

> › Do you feel alone and wish for help from your soul team? Are your efforts to "be an adult" blocking your connection? How might you open yourself up energetically to invite them in?

> › Make a list of the times when you felt the presence of Spirit. Write about what that experience felt like.

> › Can you remember a time when you trusted your gut? When you didn't? Jot what happened as a result of that trust, or lack of trust.

WHAT SPIRIT WANTS YOU TO KNOW

Experiences and emotions can stay with you for decades, but that is not always in your best interest. Some energy is not meant for you to hold on to. For example, if you were betrayed by your best friend in high school, you might be extra aware of red flags when meeting new people. It's okay to be aware, but don't let one bad experience rob you of the ability to trust. Everyone is not the same! You can still be open to friendship and love, and experience many warm, fulfilling relationships. Open your heart and trust your intuition. Your guides and angels are there to guide you to achieve your true destiny. You can release the energy of the past when you learn to trust in their guidance.

Chapter 3

THE CHALLENGE OF LIFE
AND LESSONS LEARNED

People often think of youth as a carefree time, but although babies and young children don't have the same responsibilities and stresses that adults do, they are more vulnerable to their environment and the people in their lives. Even if they don't understand it in a conscious sense, these sensitive young souls are affected by the negative energy around them, and it can stick with them and cause problems for years—even decades.

If you were exposed to trauma as a child, you might find as you move through life that your pain, if not addressed, becomes like an anchor, holding you back. Even with the help of your spirit team, you'll have a hard time moving forward and fulfilling your destiny unless you learn to process those old feelings and emotions.

In this chapter, we'll explore the stored childhood experiences that, unexamined, can cling to you for a lifetime. I'll share some helpful insights I've learned from my communication with the spirit people. This knowledge will empower you to process and shed that energy so you can move forward, unburdened, to learn the lessons you need for fulfilling the destiny you mapped out before you started your earthly journey.

PATTERNS CAN BE ROOTED EARLY IN LIFE . . .
OR EVEN BEFORE YOU WERE BORN

Children are born young, innocent, and pure, with a strong connection to heaven. As they start to get older, earthly things like money, ambition, jealousy, and lust can dilute their spiritual connection.

Here on earth, situations are put in your path that can generate anxiety, fear, and insecurity. Some of these events begin in your own lifetime, but others are passed down through generations. As I've said before, children are like sponges, not just when they're picking up bad words and phrases, but also when it comes to absorbing energy.

That's why after being exposed to a parent's dysfunctional relationship as a child, that energy may cling to you and cause you to avoid or subconsciously sabotage relationships as an adult.

It may not have started with your parents. As you examine your history, you may realize that your parents learned their behavior from their parents, and so on. Anger, jealousy, and insecurity are passed down through generations, as are alcoholism and other addictions. But you're not destined to continue living with the mistakes of your parents and grandparents. With help from your soul team, you can break the cycle. In fact, doing so may be an important part of your life's purpose. The lessons and insights you gain from observing the challenges of others can be the keys that unlock your best life.

EVERYTHING YOU EXPERIENCE IS
PART OF A MASTER PLAN

No matter what age you are, you can never entirely avoid pain and negative energy. In fact, you shouldn't even try, because those experiences, good and bad, are part of your journey. Life is filled with twists and turns, lessons and milestones. Throughout your life, your guides will put opportunities in front of you that have the potential to help you grow. Although they will do their best to nudge you in the right direction, ultimately you are responsible for how you behave and the choices that you make.

What Happens May Not Be Under Your Control,
but How You React Is Your Decision

Everyone faces challenges in their life, and some of them can cast a big shadow for years to come. You've probably experienced some of these situations in your own life or observed them in others:

› Some adults are afraid of dogs because they were
  bitten or frightened by a dog when they were younger.
  They may inherit that fear even if they were never
  personally harmed. If your mom was bitten by a dog,
  she might be overprotective and imprint her fear upon
  you by conveying the message *Dogs are dangerous.*

› When you watch your mother or someone you know struggle to leave an abusive relationship, it can reinforce a message that you need to protect yourself from getting close to someone romantically.

› The trauma of having a miscarriage (or knowing someone who had one) can make you fearful that you'll never have children. You might avoid even trying because the potential for pain is too great.

› Maybe your parents couldn't pay the bills, leaving you with a scarcity mentality. A whole generation of people that grew up during the Depression lived under the shadow of financial insecurity for decades, even when they had good jobs and money in the bank.

› Fears related to water are common and may be rooted in anything from childhood baths, a scary experience at the beach or pool, even "Shark Week" on the Discovery Channel. I had a friend who internalized her mom's warning to avoid swimming after eating to the point that she avoided beaches and pools altogether.

› As we've discussed, divorce or abandonment by a parent can scar a child in all kinds of ways, often encouraging them to put up protective "walls" to avoid intimacy as an adult.

› Observing someone close to you struggle with health issues can leave you with concerns about your own health—and make you overly cautious about the smallest bruise or sniffle.

› When a parent dies young, often their children will consciously or subconsciously believe that their lives will also end prematurely. This fear of an early demise can affect the long-term choices they make about everything from their career and investments to getting married and having children of their own.

› No one wants to be injured in an accident, but if you see danger everywhere you look and do everything you can to avoid getting hurt, it's almost guaranteed that you'll miss out on some fun, positive experiences.

› Some people fear people who are different from them. This energy is often a by-product of your early environment or the people who raised you. Only spending time with people who are "like you" is like spending your life in a box. It limits your perspective and keeps you from growing and experiencing more in life.

› If you're overly worried about what people think of you, or if you have experienced bullying in your life, it can keep you from making new friends. I understand the urge to protect yourself by building walls and keeping people away—but that also robs you of the chance to meet people who you might truly connect with. My advice? Don't assume all people are the same, and let people show you who they are instead of judging them before you get to know them.

Whether they come from things you've been told, observed, or actually experienced, fears like these have one thing in common—subconsciously, they are being kept alive by you. Yes, they're a way of avoiding pain, but they also hold you back from taking risks, having a full life, and experiencing new things.

As you grow, you become more aware and in control of what's happening around you, and gain a stronger sense of your own identity. Now that you're not a dependent child, you learn ways to protect yourself from the energy of others, even if that means leaving the room or blocking someone on your phone. Because you're no longer powerless, watching your parents argue at twenty feels different than it did when you were six.

But you still have to address the "old stuff"—the experiences, beliefs, and fears that you still carry with you. They can be the root cause of the fear, anxiety, and discomfort you feel in certain situations.

DECLUTTERING YOUR SPIRITUAL "HOUSE" AND CLEARING OUT YOUR PSYCHE

Alexa and I love to clear out and purge our house and garage. Every time we take this on, it makes us feel lighter and happier in our surroundings and gives us more space to grow. Not only that, but going through our belongings and donating what we no longer need gives us a renewed appreciation for the things we decide to keep.

"Spring cleaning" your soul is just as satisfying. Your body is your temple and spiritual house. Like your physical home, it contains things that are important to you. In both your physical and spiritual home, there are sentimental keepsakes as well as necessities for day-to-day life. But imagine if you kept everything you ever brought into your home and never threw anything out. Soon there would be no room to move—your possessions would pile up and block the sun, and even could present a health hazard. Do not become a hoarder for your soul!

Handling Things Once

I talked to a professional organizer once, and they told me that to maximize productivity, every piece of paper that comes across your desk and every email that enters your inbox should be handled just once. Read it and address it, then scan it, file it, or throw it away. It's the same thing when you experience pain or trauma. You have to see it for what it is, find the lesson, and let it go.

As humans, sometimes we want to keep handling things so we can make them come out perfect—it can be a relationship, a job, or anything that we're stuck on. If we can't resolve the issue to our satisfaction, we may choose to push it down and pack it away. This kind of "emotional hoarding" can hold us back in life.

When issues go unresolved, they can clutter your psyche. Let's go back to the situation where your parents were always fighting, and it taught you to fear conflict. You were powerless to change that as a child, and you can't go back in time as an adult and fix the past. If you hang on to that experience without learning from it, it will keep you from being your best in relationships, jobs, and just about every area of your life.

But how can you unwrap and examine something that affected you so strongly in the past that you hid it away and avoided even thinking about it? The secret is detachment. Detachment gives you the ability to step back, look back with clear eyes, and see things for what they are without taking them personally.

Practicing detachment can be easier said than done, but it's worth the effort. When you're struggling to "let go and move on," it helps to remember these three things:

1. What happened really wasn't about you. Everyone is dealing with their own fears, insecurities, and baggage. That doesn't make the fact that someone hurt you in the past right, but it helps you look back on the situation with compassion as you remind yourself that their behavior and the way they treated you was a reflection on them, not on you!

2. There's a lesson in everything. If you look back and realize that an unpleasant experience taught you something or made you stronger and more resilient, you will start seeing yourself as someone who rose above adversity, rather than being a victim.

3. You attract what you focus on. I'm not saying to erase everything bad from your memory—you can't, and pushing things down isn't a good idea. However, if you spend more time thinking about happy events and people who treated you well, the bad memories will have a lot less power over you, and you'll attract more of the good things.

Staying Attached When You Know
You Should Let Go

Sometimes we have to release what no longer fits into your life, even if it was meaningful to you at one time. When I moved into my first house, I bought a beautiful dining room set. It was the first real furniture I'd ever bought, and I was so proud of it. The set came with a large, ornate hutch that I filled with my favorite china and crystal pieces. The hutch was gorgeous, but it overpowered the space. I was in denial about it, until a designer friend urged me to get rid of it. She told me that it made the room unbalanced, and that the space would look so much better without it.

I was so mad! I had spent so much money on this piece of furniture, and I loved it. But I couldn't deny what was right in front of my eyes. My beautiful hutch didn't work in the space, and it was interfering with our enjoyment of the room. After a few days I made the hard choice and let it go. Now when we have people over, everyone can push their chairs back and spread out, and the room is so much more inviting and functional.

When you hold on to things past the point where you should, or push down emotions you don't want to deal with, it clogs your energy and holds you back from being the person you were born to be. But that's not the only thing that can keep you from moving forward in your life. Sometimes it's not just trauma that we hold on to. People can cling to positive events and times in their lives too.

When Time Stands Still . . .

In my twenties I started to notice that many people I knew who had been very popular and successful in high school weren't doing much with

49

their lives after graduation. I'd run into a classmate who had been a top athlete, head cheerleader, honor student, voted most popular or most likely to succeed, and it was as if time had stood still for them and all they could talk about was high school. I got the sense that they'd peaked in high school and were now stuck reliving their glory days. It made me realize that not moving on from a positive part of your life can slow you down just as much as refusing to move on from a traumatic experience. It's like I said earlier about only touching every piece of paper or email that comes across your desk once. It doesn't matter if it's a bill, a check, or a postcard. If you don't deal with things as they come, it can make you less productive, and less able to move forward.

Personal Filters Color Our Perception

Sometimes in relationships you see the other person through your own filter. You might just see their potential, or who you wish they were. You may have misread them totally in the past, and still be clinging to an idealized image of them. That can be bad if you are with someone who is in a downward spiral or is actually not the person you believe them to be. If you don't see someone for who they actually are, it's hard to make a relationship work.

WISDOM I'VE PICKED UP FROM HEAVEN

Life is a series of learning experiences that provide you with the opportunity to embrace a new version of your life. I want to share some things I've learned from souls in heaven to help you face your fears and live your best life possible.

So let's take a minute to unpack these important points. These ideas will help you to process painful life events (from your recent past and your childhood) so you can learn and grow from them:

› Everything that happened to you isn't yours to hold on to.

› You can't always control what happens to you, but you can control how you react.

› Just because you've had some bad luck doesn't mean you deserved it, or that it's your destiny.

› It is your choice whether your fear holds you back or propels you forward. For example, if one day you get pulled under the waves at the beach and it scares you, you can choose to not swim at the beach again, or you can take lessons and become a stronger swimmer so you feel safer in the water.

› Don't let past trauma define you. You're more than your pain— so get out there and be open to experiencing things.

› Make processing, healing, and purging pain a positive part of your life. Talk to a friend or a therapist, or even journal—but with the intent of processing, learning, and moving on.

Keep in mind that if everyone just focused on the pain in life, no one would ever do anything. Everything has a downside. Friends can let you down, children keep you up at night, pets pee on the carpet and die way too young, relationships require compromise and can end painfully, things at home can break down and need replacing, jobs can be stressful and all-consuming. Remember, the kind of pain that comes from doing things and taking risks is so much more productive and rewarding than the pain that comes from avoiding things.

LIFE IS HARD, BUT YOU CAN CHOOSE THE KIND OF HARD YOU WANT

A teacher friend of mine, named Alex, recently told her students that there are two types of difficulty.

Alex shared the important lesson she teaches each class of new students. She was struck with this insight after noticing some of the children in her class complaining that things "came easy" to some people.

Here's what she tells her students:

"Life is always going to be hard—and you get to choose your hard. Life is hard when you don't have an education or goals. Life is hard when you decide not to study, practice, and put the work in. If you don't try, you won't do well at school, sports, or your job. And that's hard. But it's also hard being successful, because that requires responsibility and sacrifice. Being wealthy is hard, and being poor is hard. Struggling to pay your bills is hard, and being a CEO is hard. When you don't realize that, you tend to envy people because they don't have your struggles, but they have their own. Maybe they don't have to get up early and commute to work, but also don't get the rewards of a paycheck and the fulfillment of a career.

"The moral of this is everyone has struggles, everyone has pain. You can't avoid pain, but you can take control of your destiny."

Next time you find yourself in a difficult situation, feeling sorry for yourself, or afraid to take a chance, remember the wise words Alex shares with her students, and embrace life's hardships and learn from them.

*Divorce Can Open Your Eyes, and What You Learn Can
Lead You to a Brighter Future*

A healthy, fulfilling relationship can be the source of so much happiness. The flip side of this is that relationships can also end and bring you pain. After a breakup or divorce, it's easy to look back and hate your ex. After all, you entered into a partnership with high hopes and expectations, only to have it end in conflict and regrets. But if you see that relationship for what it was—a part of your life's journey—you'll realize that you benefited along the way. While you were married, you may have explored new places, had children, made friends, and advanced in your career. You may have resolved childhood issues and grown as a person. This is one area where detachment can serve you well. If you step back and acknowledge what you gained, you'll find it easier to move on without bitterness.

When it comes to love and marriage, the most important thing to realize is that you can't change people, you can only change yourself. I used to think that if you found your soul mate, nothing could go wrong! You'd automatically be together for life and beyond. Well, part of that is true. You will reunite with your soul mate in heaven, but you may not be able to make a relationship work here on earth. You might fall in love with your soul mate and along the way something happens—an affair, addiction, or an unforeseen circumstance—that makes them unrecognizable and causes the relationship to fail.

KEEP AN OPEN MIND AND A POSITIVE ATTITUDE

I wanted to share this story to prove that the saying "Fool me once, shame on you; fool me twice, shame on me" doesn't always apply. Dave is a friend of mine who owns a very successful restaurant in Rhode Island. He told me about an encounter he had with a homeless man who was hanging out at the dumpster. He saw that the man looked hungry, so he went into the kitchen and put together a delicious three-course meal of salad, pasta, and chicken parmesan. He got everything warm and ready for the man and brought it out to him. The next week, he saw the same man in front of his restaurant. He greeted the man, but to his shock, the man started screaming at him, "Your food sucks!"

A few weeks later, a different man came into the restaurant and asked to talk to the owner. "I'm so embarrassed, but I'm hungry, down on my luck, and could really use a hot meal." Dave didn't think twice, and put together a meal for the man, who ate it hungrily and left. A month later, that second man came back into the restaurant and came up to my friend. "That little bit of hope transformed my life," he said. "After I ate that meal and experienced your kindness, I felt so much better that I decided to get myself a job." The grateful man wanted to pay for the meal, but Dave wouldn't hear of it, so he promised to be a loyal customer for life. When Dave told me this story, he couldn't stop saying how glad he was that he didn't put up walls after his negative experience with the first man.

SPIRIT GUIDES—
YOUR NAVIGATION SYSTEM FROM HEAVEN

In this chapter, I encourage you to see things for what they really are, which includes facing the facts when it comes to your past and your relationships. When you do this, you allow your spirit guides to do their job—which is to guide you on your path. Remember, your guides will put opportunities in front of you. Thanks to them, you will explore career options, meet people who will play an important role in your life, and work through challenges that shape who you are. People worry a lot about not seeing signs from their guides and missing out on their big chance. As long as you're not too guarded, afraid, or bogged down in the past, your guides will be able to do their job!

Don't spend too much time focusing on missed opportunities. I believe that if something is meant to be, it will be. Opportunity always comes back around, and what's meant for you will happen if you're in the right place to receive it.

For example, people thought I was crazy for turning down TV opportunities. I had so many calls from different television networks wanting to do shows about ghost hunting and the paranormal; however, it just didn't feel like the right fit for me and I had to trust my intuition and pass. I was so happy that I listened to my intuition when the opportunity came back around and presented itself to me in a different way with a different show. It just goes to show that when something is meant for you, it will present itself in different ways and at different points of your life.

When you're in a situation that's challenging for you, here are some questions to ask your guides and yourself:

> Why was I presented with this situation?

> What lesson is there to learn?

> Why does this have such an emotional, triggering charge for me?

> Am I taking this experience too personally?

› What is the best way to grow from this?

› What are my options?

Sometimes you might have a bad experience simply because you're new to something. If you get in over your head the first time, you have a choice. You can make sure you never jump into an intimidating situation like that again, or you can learn from the experience and prepare better the next time. Here's something that happened to me that perfectly illustrates that point.

A SHOCKING EXPERIENCE

Years ago, I was invited to be on my first radio show. My agent set it up early in my career, at a time when I was inexperienced and didn't know what to expect or how to prepare. Boy, did I learn some lessons that day!

The radio show was hosted by a popular shock jock. You probably know that this kind of host doesn't get listeners by being nice and polite. The entire hour I was there, he asked questions designed to belittle me and cracked jokes. I was so freaked out that I didn't even know how to answer the questions. I froze, and I wound up laughing nervously, unable to answer his questions. He put on quite a show, and if he was trying to make me look like a fool, he succeeded.

Afterward, I called my publicist and said, "NEVER AGAIN!"

That's when she gave me a big dose of reality. "This is your path, Matt, and you're going to encounter skeptics over and over."

"You have to go on the show again," she said.

"What? No way!" I said.

But she convinced me and scheduled another radio spot with the same host.

This time I prepared, and it was like night and day compared to the first interview.

Did I change this shock jock's mind? No, but I gave him some things to think about, and I was proud of the way I answered his questions.

What was much more important than convincing him was how my words resonated with his audience. I got great feedback from people, and many listeners called me after the show to sign up for readings. In spite of my initial embarrassment, I had learned from the first experience, reminded myself (or my publicist reminded me) that this was my path, and focused on sharing my message of heaven and the afterlife.

Another thing I realized, after looking back on this experience, was that the first radio show had triggered me because of my experience of being bullied in high school. As soon as the radio host started firing questions at me, I acted like a kid because he took me right back to that place. Correction—I allowed myself to be taken back there! The second time I took control over my emotions and was prepared, and it was a totally different experience.

I was able to rewrite history, not by going back to high school and beating up the jocks, but by handling myself differently in a similar situation, and getting my power back.

LETTING GO OF ANGER

During a reading, souls will often talk about how after their death, the sons and daughters they left behind stopped talking to each other. It might have been because one was resentful because they'd shouldered most of the responsibility for the dying parent, or it may have had to do with the estate. Either way, you'd be shocked at how often this comes up (or maybe you wouldn't be shocked!).

I remember one reading where a woman with a dying mother felt guilty that she couldn't get her brother to come to the hospital because her mother desperately wanted to see him before she passed. She felt anger at his behavior and resentment that all the responsibility had fallen on her. After her mother passed, she came through to me in a reading. She told her daughter that she shouldn't let those feelings cloud the beautiful time they had spent together in those last days. This is another example of the "kinds of hard." The brother had to deal with his own guilt and loss, and the daughter had all the responsibility but benefited from the love she shared with her mom. Would it have been great if her brother was with her? YES, but we can't control other people. We can only do what is right for us.

CONQUERING YOUR PAIN

Here's another reading, and another example of how people limit themselves in order to avoid pain.

I met with a woman who had lost her fiancé to an overdose. She thought he had overcome his addiction, so his death totally shocked her. He had sworn to her every day that he was okay and that he wasn't using. When they got engaged, he promised her that the addiction was behind him and that if he ever relapsed, he would be truthful with her. Unfortunately he lied. She woke up one day to find him dead on the bathroom floor. She was shattered, not only by his death, but by the fact that she had been completely blindsided. From that moment, she found herself stuck and unable to move on.

This experience caused her so much pain that she gave up on her dreams of getting married and having children, and let herself become completely swallowed up in grief. Fortunately when she came to me for a reading her fiancé came through. He was filled with regret, because he could clearly see how his addiction had ruined her life. But during his life review, he'd had time to reflect on his actions, and he had some valuable advice for her. He told her that the pain she was feeling came from him. He said that you can't control other people's choices (stop me if you've heard that before), but that she had the power to choose for herself. He begged her not to allow his choice to affect her happiness and to destroy her dream of being a mom and having a family. Over and over, he reminded her that he'd made his choice, which had turned out badly. Now she had to make hers. She could let his mistake ruin her life, or she could continue on her pathway and go after what she wanted.

Until her fiancé came through in our reading, the woman had felt powerless. But hearing his words, she realized she had a choice and that it was up to her to rebuild her life. She made the hard decision to put herself back out there, and when she did, she found a new love to go with her new way of looking at life.

SPIRITUAL PRACTICE

Exercise: Clearing Out the Baggage

I'm going to have you do something that might not seem very "spiritual" at first. But believe me, it will be! First, pick a closet, an area of the garage, even a drawer, and clean it out.

As you go through each item, think of its significance in your life. Ask yourself:

› When was the last time you used this?

› Does this item bring you happiness or still serve a purpose?

› Is this item associated with happy memories?

› Is there a reason why you are holding on to this item?

If the item is not serving a purpose in your life, get rid of it. A good rule of thumb I always say to Alexa is that if we have not used something in over a year, it needs to go.

You can also donate those items that you have a hard time throwing away. It might help you part with something if you know that someone in need will put it to good use. Imagining your unwanted possessions being appreciated and helping someone else feels so good!

Now for the spiritual part. Pick a section of "emotional baggage" to clean out. Meditate for a few minutes and think about a time in your life when you felt powerless, unsafe, or afraid.

Maybe you were bullied in school, had an abusive parent, or struggled with an illness. You'll know you have the right memory when it triggers feelings of sadness or anger when you revisit it. Now take out a journal and fully explore your feelings. Write down what happened, how you felt at the time, and list the ways this event still affects you today. Let yourself fully explore the experience, and when you're done, jot down the lessons you learned. Take a deep breath and release the pain by exhaling and sending those negative thoughts to heaven and your angels. Repeat to yourself, "The pain and past is no longer with me, just the life lesson."

For the next couple of days, just hold that knowledge of what you learned inside you. Then open up your journal again and invite your guides to join you as you write down some ways that you are wiser, stronger, and more resilient because of what happened. The goal of this is to fully unpack your trauma, then let it go and allow awareness and gratitude to take its place.

WHAT SPIRIT WANTS YOU TO KNOW

Look back on your life and consider how your challenges have shaped and affected you. Acknowledge that you would not be the person you are today without having gone through those challenges. Step back and revisit the experience with detachment. You are not to blame for things that happened when you were young and inexperienced, but you have the power to release that pain so you can live life to the fullest.

Chapter 4

BECOME YOUR OWN SUCCESS STORY

If you've read this far, you know that unexplored emotions and traumatic experiences can keep you stuck if you don't process them. You understand that letting go of old, negative energy can be hard, but it's worth the effort because it makes space in your life for exciting new opportunities.

Now for the fun part. In this chapter I'll share insights from Spirit and provide you with techniques for you to realize your dreams and enjoy an abundance of love, happiness, security, and success. You'll learn how to ask for help from your guides, angels, and loved ones in heaven. Best of all, you'll gain an understanding of a powerful force called divine flow that will allow you to manifest and attract everything you desire.

LET'S TALK ABOUT "DIVINE FLOW"

Learning to align with heaven through thoughts, actions, intentions, and positive expectations creates a natural flow to transform your life . . . this is divine flow.

Something I tell people that is a *big* surprise: Your loved ones on the other side are creating and living the lives they wished they could have lived here. They do inspirational work—unimaginably magnificent, creative, incredible things.

The difference is that in heaven, they have no fears or doubts or limitations. They are in divine flow. Here on earth we are trying to come as close to that as possible, but it's difficult. There are so many physical worries and obstacles that block us from pursuing our true passions and purpose.

We all have the ability to create the lives we wish; whether you live in heaven or on earth, it is our birthright. Imagine being born with a road map in your hands. Well, you do have one. It's called divine flow.

Getting into the Flow

The first step toward achieving your goals is deciding exactly what you want. Everyone's idea of a successful, fulfilling life looks a little bit different, so how do you know when you've figured out your true path? Here's a hint. When you're in the right place, the universe responds by opening doors and putting the right people and opportunities in front of you. In this chapter I'll be sharing stories, including my own, that illustrate this point.

You Were Born to Live an Extraordinary Life

I have wonderful news! There are opportunities written in the stars that are meant for you and nobody else. Spirit tells me that we are all born with divine skills and abilities to help us achieve our unique purpose and fulfill our destiny. Before you're born, your guides, angels, and loved ones in heaven help you create a road map for your time on earth. As you go through life, you'll learn how to use your gifts to navigate the obstacles and opportunities you encounter.

Expect Delays, Surprises, and Challenges

Like any trip you take, no matter how thoroughly you plan things out in advance, once you're on your way, unexpected events can pop up and surprise you. Even during a short weekend getaway, you may find yourself delayed by car trouble, missed flights, bad weather, illness, or a variety of other events. As you journey through life, you can expect to encounter more challenges that have the potential to interfere with your progress or pull you off course. Before you get discouraged, here are two things to keep in mind. First, your guides, angels, and loved ones in heaven are there to protect you and steer you in the right direction. In addition, there are some simple techniques you can learn and use to stay on track and write your own success story.

Don't Give Up on Your Dreams

If you're not happy with where you are in life, know that you have the power to turn things around. In countless conversations, souls in heaven have told me that as long as you're living and breathing, you still have the chance to pursue your dreams and make the most of the precious time you have on earth.

Earlier we talked about how so many people hold on to trauma and limiting beliefs from their past. As you pursue your life's purpose, suppressed feelings and negative energy can be like tethers, keeping you shackled to your pain. It may be hard to revisit the traumatic experiences you've been trying so hard to forget, but doing so is the key to releasing that energetic anchor and realizing your dreams. And remember, even if the road is difficult, you don't have to travel it alone. Your spirit team is with you every step of the way.

Loved Ones in Heaven Don't Want You to
Make the Same Mistakes They Did

Unlike your angels, your loved ones in heaven and spirit guides have experienced their own lifetime on earth, which puts them in a good position to help you avoid missing out on opportunities and winding up with regrets. Many of them know what that's like firsthand, because they've already gone through their life review and been able to see the effects of their own choices and behavioral patterns. They have total clarity about the mistakes they made while they were alive, and are in a position to do something about it.

In fact, those souls are busy embracing their true essence. In heaven, they have the opportunity to tap into their gifts to do inspirational work.

Souls are able to achieve things in the afterlife that are so magnificent we can barely imagine them. The act of crossing over and entering heaven, along with the insights gained in their life review, forces them to release self-doubt and limiting beliefs, and as souls in heaven, they have access to the infinite source of universal wisdom.

As long as you have the courage to face your fears and maintain a strong connection to your spirit team, you won't have to wait until you're dead to do great things. Just as limiting beliefs don't exist in heaven, they don't have to exist while you're alive. And there's no group more qualified and dedicated to helping you move past them than your guides, angels, and loved ones in heaven.

WHAT MAKES YOU SPECIAL?

One of the things I've learned from Spirit, as well as from observing everyone around me, is that people don't always realize what makes them great.

Some people are born to be painters, some musicians. Some are born teachers, inventors, or leaders. I was fortunate enough to be able to communicate with the dead. That's a pretty specific gift, but if you can't readily identify your uniqueness, just think back to what you love. What conversations or activities excite you most? Is there something you are better at than anyone else you know? When you spend time doing something you love, time disappears as you become completely one with your creation.

Your passion might turn into a career, but it doesn't have to. There are many ways to share what you have in your heart to benefit yourself and others.

When you follow your heart, embrace your talents, skills, and abilities, and are on your life path, heaven helps you to reach success. It all flows naturally and doors just seem to open.

ENCOURAGEMENT FROM BEYOND

When someone passes, they will often come back in a reading to give a friend or family member the benefit of their insights.

I remember one reading vividly, because it perfectly illustrates how souls can help their loved ones benefit from what they learned in heaven. There were two friends who were both incredibly talented songwriters and singers. They loved spending time together creating music and performing for themselves. They shared their songs with a few friends, but never could summon up the confidence to perform in public. When one of the friends passed, he realized that he had deprived himself, his friend, and the world by not taking the leap and sharing his musical gifts. He came through to me in a reading, and begged me to tell his friend not to make the same mistake. She realized that he had died without sharing his music with the world, and now she had the chance to do it for both of them. His message had such a powerful effect on her! She told me she was going to seek out opportunities to perform in public, and I could see that the message from her friend in heaven had been the motivation she needed to break through the barriers and achieve the success she deserved.

Follow Your Heart

In the last example, you saw how a lack of confidence prevented a talented musician from sharing his music with the world. He and his partner allowed fear to hold them back, and it wasn't until his passing that he was able to see how he had cheated himself and his partner by doing so.

Let's explore the limiting beliefs you create for yourself. These fear-based thoughts can deprive you of success and happiness, but you don't have to let them.

Do you ever find yourself thinking that you're too old, too broke, not cute enough, not athletic enough, not tall enough, not smart enough, not (fill in the blank) enough, to take a chance or try something new? Maybe you tell yourself that you don't have the support you need, or remind yourself of a time when you failed before. Where do these thoughts come from? They come from the most human part of you: your brain! Your mind has a way of working overtime to help you avoid the things you fear most, like failure, pain, disappointment, and the judgment of other people. In a misguided effort to protect you, your brain says no a lot! But sometimes you have to follow your heart, which might mean taking a risk and facing your fears to get what you want.

You might be thinking to yourself, *I'm pretty confident, and I don't believe my thoughts hold me back.* That may be true, but I encourage you to dig a little deeper. Limiting beliefs don't have to be anything drastic. Just about every human being has a level of fear and insecurity that holds them back to some degree. This can manifest itself in something as simple as not having the confidence to take a risk, or worrying too much about pleasing others instead of pursuing your own dreams.

Guides Can Only Help You If You Let Them

Think of all the times you said no or put something off because of fear. Sometimes you don't realize how much you're missing out on until someone points it out to you.

A friend of mine came to me and she was frustrated that she couldn't meet her soul mate. Her situation was kind of unique. She had built a successful career but, because of her social anxiety, had arranged her life in such a way that she only left home to walk to the grocery store. Although she was often invited to conferences and events related to work, she found reasons to turn them all down. She never put herself on a dating site, and even avoided in-person family functions. Despite the fact that her guides put multiple opportunities to branch out and meet people in front of her, she kept her windows shut and her door locked, and barricaded herself, literally and spiritually, inside her home so she didn't have to face her fears.

I asked if I could do a reading for her, hoping that her guides would have some good advice. They immediately relayed the message that they could only go so far, and that she had to break out of the cage she'd created for herself with her fear and anxiety. She heard them, and agreed to make more of an effort to put herself out into the world. I heard from her a few months later, and she couldn't wait to share the news that she was dating someone she had met at a work function.

Your guides can provide valuable support, but you have to be open to taking their advice. It's like hiring a consultant. You have to first share your goals and challenges with that consultant so they can make a good recommendation, then you have to drop your defenses and fears and take their advice. Your spirit team is better than most consultants, because they can see what's best for you with perfect clarity and have the power to help make it happen.

Pushing Through Limits With
Your Spirit Team

Once you understand where your thoughts and worries come from, you can make the changes you need to move forward. Remember, just as limiting beliefs don't exist in heaven, they don't have to exist while you're alive. And there's no group more qualified and dedicated to helping you move past them than your spirit team.

Your spirit guides are there to keep you on track and moving in the right direction. They'll make sure your path crosses with people who will help you achieve your purpose. Your loved ones in heaven are watching over you too, and will do whatever they can to make sure you don't repeat the mistakes they made.

I remember the day that a soul came through in a reading with such inspiring words for his daughter. Since she was a child, she had always been passionate about cooking, and at the time of the reading, was wondering if she should leave a safe, boring office job to accept the position of chef at a new restaurant that was opening up in town. Her father encouraged her to take the leap, and shared these words: "What if you said yes to any opportunity that could get you closer to what you desire—how different would your life be?"

That simple question opened her eyes, and mine! In fact, it got me thinking about some of the reasons people say no.

Do any of these excuses sound familiar?

› I'm just too practical to give up my security and take a chance.

› What would happen if I fail?

› I'm just waiting for the right time!

› I have too many other people to take care of, their needs have to come first.

You can always find an excuse or a reason not to make a move toward something. It might be risky, and it might not be something that everyone in your life understands or supports. If your spouse, parents, or children are questioning your choices, listen to what they have to say, but keep in mind that no one knows what's right for you—not even the people who love you most. Their hearts may be in the right place, but at the end of the day it's your own heart you have to listen to. I remember how good it felt when I decided to be an EMT. It was just the first step in my career journey, and it was also the first time I really understood that I had to make my own choices in life, even if it meant disappointing my parents. Here's what happened . . .

HOW I BECAME A PSYCHIC MEDIUM

I was never good in school. I only went to college because my parents expected me to. However, once I was there, I never felt that I belonged. I started getting depressed because I believed I would never be as smart as the other kids, and I wasn't good at studying or taking tests. My thoughts would wander, I would get anxious, and I could never sit still. Not to mention, my psychic ability had me reading the room instead of the textbooks! I saw everyone around me deciding to be doctors, lawyers, and nurses, and I felt trapped in the crowd.

I decided to drop out of college and enrolled in a trade school to become an emergency medical technician (EMT). I'd always felt a deep compassion for others, and I really wanted to help people to heal and to make a difference. Little did I know that I would wind up helping and healing people, but not from the back of an ambulance!

It wasn't easy telling my parents that I wanted to drop out of college and become an EMT. They were furious. They told me I would have to pay my own way since I had already wasted their money on a semester that I never finished. I enrolled in the next session of EMT school and signed up for classes.

Wow! It was like someone had flipped a switch. Suddenly I had no problem paying attention in class. I was enthralled by what I was learning and loved the personal interactions and hands-on experiences. Not to mention, my psychic ability this time helped me as I could use my abilities to sense and feel people on a deeper level.

For once in my life I was acing tests, flying through exams, and truly enjoying being in the classroom. Everything flowed easily and naturally. Somehow what I was learning seemed intuitive, and I felt I was at the right place at the right time.

Becoming an EMT was a wonderful experience. I was having a great time, unaware that I was moving closer to my true purpose, when an unexpected coincidence occurred.

When I was in training, I got close to a partner I was assigned to and started opening up about my psychic gifts and abilities. In doing so I learned that she, too, was a medium and was drawn to the EMT work to help others to heal. What were the odds of that happening? For once in my life I was meeting someone who was like me, and who understood what I was going through.

This amazing coincidence gave me the courage to speak out about my gift, and learn more about it. I took all of this as a sign that Spirit was paving a pathway for me. My ongoing conversations with my EMT partner helped open my eyes to what I really wanted, and as much as I loved being an EMT, my destiny was elsewhere.

Following Your Dreams Is Hard,
But It's the Best Kind of Hard Ever

It's scary to give up your predictable, comfortable routine to pursue a bigger dream, but I'm here to tell you it's worth the risk. When I think about where I am today, I'm so grateful! I could easily have spent the first thirty years of my life checking all the boxes, going to college, becoming an emergency medical technician (EMT), maybe buying a house or a condo. I had friends and a job I liked, I was saving money, and life was fine.

But one fateful day, a friend took me to see a psychic medium who told me that my gift would help and heal people. At that point I knew I had to take a chance on an extraordinary life. How was I so sure this was my destiny? Well, the medium gave me a pretty good clue, but I could easily have discounted what she said. I didn't, because her words resonated deep in my soul and confirmed so many feelings I'd had throughout my life. I had been connected to Spirit as a child and often received messages from people who had passed over. Despite my mom's support, that experience was a lot for a child to handle. As I got older, I just wanted to be a normal teenager, so I pushed my gift away. My encounter with the medium was an invitation to rediscover my mediumship gift. It was like a bolt of lightning, illuminating what had been hidden in my subconscious! Suddenly I knew without a shadow of a doubt that mediumship was my calling. I had always been drawn to help and heal people, and that's what inspired me to become an EMT. But it turns out, I was meant to heal people's grieving hearts and souls, not their bodies. I was born to be a medium.

Once I made the decision to practice mediumship full-time, I was all in! I started giving readings in the back of a hair salon and visiting people's homes, and word started getting around. At the same time, I prayed for the right people and opportunities to be put in my path, and Spirit came through for me. Within a very short time, I met my agent, and we pushed forward together. It wasn't always easy, but the opportunities kept coming, and I learned from every one of them. As my success grew, I became more and more confident that I was on the right path. Looking back, I realize that the medium who told me about my gift, my spirit team, and my own commitment to my goal helped me to achieve and sustain a state of realizing my true potential.

MEETING YOUR SOUL MATE

When imagining your best life, it's likely that career isn't the only thing you think of. For most people, having someone to share their success with is an essential part of their life's plan. That's where a soul mate comes in!

We all want to meet our twin flame, the person we're destined to be with for life. Your guides will do their best to make sure you cross paths with your soul mate, but there's a lot that can get in the way. For example, you might already be in a relationship with someone who is not your soul mate. Your mind or your ego might be doing its best to convince you this person is "the one." They may be great-looking and successful, and you might be flattered that they're interested in you. But that doesn't mean they're your soul mate. The attraction may be there, but there might also be a million red flags that your guides are showing you, and you choose to ignore them.

Because finding your soul mate is so important, I recommend doing some soul-searching when you meet someone new to make sure you're seeing the whole picture. I put together some attributes that don't have anything to do with looks, money, or sex. They made sense for me, and if you're looking for your soul mate, you may want to use them, and also add some more items that resonate with you.

When asking these questions and considering how your new

relationship stacks up, make sure you tune in to your heart and your intuition. Imagine your future with this person, and call upon your guides and angels to weigh in on these important topics:

> Does he or she have the personal traits that are most important to me in a significant other?

> Can I imagine this person in the role of husband or wife?

> Do I see this person as someone who will be a good parent?

> Will this person be willing to navigate obstacles with me?

> Can I picture this person standing alongside me during hard times?

This might sound crazy, but I asked myself these questions at a time when I wasn't dating anyone. Why would I do that? I believe in the law of attraction, and wanted to have a clear image in my mind of who my soul mate would be in order to draw that person to me. It worked! Shortly after I went through this exercise, I met Alexa. She was everything I had imagined and more. From the day we met, our relationship was special. We could talk about anything, we had tons of things in common, and we totally got each other's sense of humor. I've never known anyone like Alexa. I'm so grateful for my past relationships, because they helped me to grow so I'd be ready when Alexa came along.

TRANSFORM YOUR LIFE: COCREATE WITH SPIRIT!

When you're moving in the right direction, you'll feel a sense of ease and harmony, as if you and the universe are pulling in the same direction.

What Is Divine Flow?

You have the ability to create the life you desire whether you live in heaven or on earth; it is your birthright. Imagine being born with a road map in your hands. Divine flow is that road map.

Your guides, angels, and loved ones in heaven are standing by to help you read your spiritual road map and achieve your dreams. With their help, you can access the divine flow, where the universe opens doors and everything falls into place. But you have to get things started.

The difference between humans and souls in heaven is that souls are free of fears, doubts, and limitations. They exist in a natural state of divine flow. Here on earth we are trying to come as close to that as possible, but it can be difficult. There are so many physical worries and obstacles that block us from pursuing our true passions and purpose.

To get in the divine flow you first must know where you're going, and focus on getting there. If you're all over the place, preoccupied with the little things you have to get done in the day, upset about a fight you had with your sister, watching the news and stressing out about things you can't control, you'll find yourself going to bed at night with the sinking feeling that you didn't get anywhere that day. Worse yet, when you're not clear about where you want to go, the universe doesn't know how to help you!

CARVING OUT A QUIET SPACE TO MANIFEST
THE LIFE OF YOUR DREAMS

Everyone is busy with the day-to-day chores and concerns of life. But when you have a clear goal and dedicate a little time to it each day, you'll be surprised how quickly things start to change.

Start by meditating or journaling for just a few minutes every morning. In that calm space, you can let go of the little distractions that keep you from seeing the path ahead of you and focus on where you want to go. Maybe you have a thought about a business you want to start or a trip you want to take. This is your time to take that thought, that little glimmer of an idea, to the next level. And guess what? When you create a clear picture in your head, or better yet, start writing a list or an outline, suddenly things start to happen.

It all starts with you. Your loved ones are watching over you from heaven. They want you to live your best life, but they're not going to push you in a direction that you're not ready to go. But when you have a clear picture of where you're going and what you want, they can help you. And that's when doors start to open and your dreams become more than just a fleeting thought.

You Don't Have to Paddle Your Own Canoe

Divine flow is when you're pulling in the same direction as your spirit team. You have a clear picture of where you want to go, and you're putting your energy toward getting there. But because you're in the flow, it isn't a struggle. You feel like someone is with you, opening doors and putting the right people in your path. They even help you navigate small day-to-day challenges by putting helpful thoughts and solutions in your head. Start the day by taking a few minutes to set your intentions and ask your guides for help. Then, at the end of the day, review and acknowledge the progress you've made, and thank your spirit team for their support and guidance.

Fitting a Square Peg in a Round Hole

When you're on the right path, and the universe and your spirit team are helping you along, everything is easy. But sometimes you get stuck. . . .

This always makes me think back to when I was a kid, and I had a big wooden puzzle game that had all different shapes cut into it. You remember those! You would have to put the round ball through the round hole and the square through the square hole and the hexagon through the hexagonal hole. When the pieces went into the right holes, they slipped through perfectly.

However, if you tried to put a square through the round hole, no matter how hard you tried, it just would not go. This is so much like life. When you're on the right pathway, heaven helps you with sending in the recruits. When you are going the wrong way, it's going to be much harder—or impossible.

SPIRITUAL PRACTICE

Exercise: Reveal and Manifest Your Deepest Desire

› Have you ever thought about what you REALLY
  wanted in life?

› Do you dream of getting married or remarried?

› Do you want to change your career or start a business?

› Do you want to improve your health or get your
  weight back on track?

Understanding what you really want in life is the first step in achieving your dreams. Here's how to open yourself up to help from the universe—and your spirit team.

Before going to bed, make your wish your mantra. For example, if you're trying to attract your soul mate, focus on the word *romance* or imagine how you want to feel in that relationship. Imagine where you would like to get married, the guests you would invite, and exactly what the ring would look like. Think about your goal for about five minutes before you go to sleep, and visualize exactly what realizing your dream would feel like. Get deep and picture all the details. Drift off to sleep with this image in your mind.

When you make it a habit to program your subconscious in this way, the signal to the spirit world becomes strong and clear. Focusing your intention before bed helps your soul do the inner work while you sleep, and the universe will get the message and help you stay in the flow—day and night!

JOURNAL PROMPT

Buy a journal, and use it to make a written record of what you want to create. Add images, drawings, quotes, whatever makes your goal feel real and concrete to you. For example, list or draw your perfect car, house, body, or feeling. Be very specific, because heaven will only respond if it understands what you desire. Be sure to write your wish in the present tense as if it is already happening. Let your imagination go wild with details! Do this for at least twenty-one days and see the magic unfold.

Understand that you are not just writing in a journal, but creating a "soul map" that you will share with heaven and hold in your heart. As you journey through life, record what happens, and update your journal with new dreams. Be sure to occasionally go back and read your entries. As you look back over the path you've traveled, you'll see how your vision and experiences have led you to the place you are today.

Chapter 5

SPIRIT'S ADVICE FOR LIVING
A LIFE WITHOUT REGRETS

There's no one better equipped to guide you on your path than someone who has lived their entire life and completed their life review in heaven. During that review, souls have the chance to look back and revisit every moment of their life to see the effects of their words and deeds. As a medium, I've had the chance to hear from people who have passed over and gone through a life review, and the information they have to share is literally life-changing. These insights were actually what inspired me to write this book. My goal is to give you the tools you need to fulfill your life purpose so you can make changes now and look back on your life and feel good about the impact you had on the world and the people around you. In the last chapter, we explored common regrets people have at the end of their lives. Now I'd like to talk about how the universe intervenes to help us change course before it's too late. Sometimes it's a near-death experience that delivers the message, but often it's a less dramatic event that triggers a much-needed correction.

Why is it so important to your guides, angels, and loved ones in heaven that you stay on your path and fulfill your destiny? Well, you're aware that your spirit team has your best interest at heart, but there's more to it than that! The lessons you learn become part of the universal knowledge bank, because when you die you take all the lessons you've learned and share them with the other souls in heaven. This information becomes part of the knowledge that all souls have access to. The more information you can gather and the more you accomplish in your life, the more you are able to contribute to that divine database.

MAKE THE MOST OF YOUR TIME ON EARTH

People sometimes say that youth is wasted on the young. I recently received a message from a soul in heaven that was a variation on that theme, and it was a great insight about what's really important in life. The message was, *Life is wasted on the living.* For as long as I've been doing readings, Spirit has let me know that many of the things we work so hard to achieve in life don't matter a bit in the afterlife. It's only when we die that we get a new perspective on how we spent our time, and how good a job we did setting priorities while we were alive.

During their life review, souls look back upon every moment of their time on earth from a new perspective. They see the mistakes they made and the opportunities they missed. While they can't go back and change what happened, they can help the living avoid making the same mistakes.

In this chapter, I'm going to share priceless wisdom I've received from souls as they look back on their lives and see the effects of their actions. People often ask if I have access to winning lottery numbers. I tell them that being a psychic medium does not give me the ability to "cheat life," but trust me, the information I'm going to share in this chapter will make a far bigger impact on your future than money. Read it carefully, because not only am I going to reveal the biggest regrets I hear from the spirit world, but I'll give you some ways to stay on your path and live a life you can look back on and be proud of.

Something happened recently that brought this point home for me:

A woman came up to me after an event and asked to book a reading to connect with her mom. I explained that I rarely do private readings anymore, but it turned out she had a bigger issue. Her mother was not actually dead yet!

I was a little confused when I realized I was being asked to connect with someone who was still alive. Then the daughter explained that her mother was very ill, and not expected to last the year.

"Mom and I have never seen eye to eye on anything. I'd like to get on your schedule in a year or so. I am certain she will have passed over by then, and I think a reading will help us understand each other."

Apparently resentment had built up between the two women for decades, and now that her mom was near death, the woman was thinking ahead. The two had so much trouble communicating that she had given up trying to resolve things while her mom was alive. She wanted to book the reading after her mother died in hopes of finally getting closure and peace.

I urged her to reconsider. I told her that since her mother was well aware that she only had a short time left on this earth, the conversation might go differently than she expected. God had given her an amazing opportunity to repair things with her mom; however, fear still held her back, and she kept pushing me to set an appointment for a reading.

It was strange for me to try to talk someone out of using my services, but I had to do it. No matter how amazing and insightful the reading might be after the woman passed over, it wouldn't be a substitute for the two women resolving their issues while both of them were still alive. I was worried that the daughter would regret her decision, and tried my hardest to convince her to take the opportunity that she had in front of her.

The whole thing kind of haunted me for a while. Sure, I deliver messages from heaven that are incredibly healing—but I've never had someone consciously choose to work through a medium when they had the option of speaking directly with their loved one while they were still alive. That would be like texting someone when they're sitting right in front of you! I felt that this woman was setting herself up for regrets, and I hope she summoned up the courage to have an honest conversation with her mother before the woman passed.

This made me think about the most common regrets that I hear in my conversations with Spirit.

TOP FIVE THINGS THE DEAD WISH THEY HAD DONE DIFFERENTLY IN LIFE

When people die, they look back with perfect hindsight and see the opportunities they missed and the mistakes they made. In the following pages, I'll share the top five regrets that come up, plus reveal the one thing that the dead never talk about.

These common regrets won't all resonate with everyone. For example, the most common thing souls wish they had done differently relates to having children. But many people have happy, fulfilling lives without children. They are comfortable with their choice while they are alive, and have no second thoughts when they pass over. But others long for children, and for one reason or another put off making it happen. Often their reasons make sense from an earthly perspective, and it's only when the soul looks back during their life review that they regret their decision.

Regret #1: Not Having Children

There are lots of reasons people put off having children. They might be caught up in their careers and be waiting for the perfect time to start a family (then run out of time), or they might struggle with infertility and are afraid to consider other options or simply give up. Some people have scars from their own childhood that make them fear being bad parents themselves.

Even when people do have babies eventually, waiting too long can cheat older members of their families out of being part of those children's lives. Here's an example of two people whose child never knew their grandmother, because they waited too long.

Missing Out on Grandma's Love

Two clients of mine have been very successful in their careers. The wife is a lawyer and the husband is a doctor. They were used to getting what they wanted, and were waiting for everything to align perfectly before starting a family. The wife set a goal for herself of making partner and made it her number one priority. She wanted to get to this elite level at her firm, and put off having a child because she was afraid it would cause her to lose her edge and not reach her career goals.

At the same time, her mother was getting up there in age and was developing some health problems. She has always supported her daughter in her career, and was so proud of her. On the other hand, she dreamed of holding her first grandchild in her arms. Despite her health issues, the mother wanted to be there to help her with the baby, but the couple kept putting off getting pregnant because there was always a career milestone to achieve first. "We'll have a baby when everything settles down," they assured everyone.

When the daughter finally got pregnant, no one was more excited than her mom! But, tragically, she died before she could hold her grandson. Suddenly my clients realized that they had their whole lives to work, that they had missed their chance to see Grandma showering love on her grandson. It hit them like a ton of bricks—holidays would be different from now on: the baby would never have the chance to taste Grandma's cooking, and there would never be the family trips and sleepovers at Grandma's that they had all looked forward to.

Make Your Dreams Happen While You Still Can

You might ask yourself how you can balance everything you want to do in life. Is it actually possible to have it all? What Spirit tells me is this: if you wait for every aspect of your life to align exactly as you want them to, you might be setting an impossible goal. If there's something you want in life, go after it when the opportunity presents itself. Remember, life is happening all around you, and you can't always have control of every detail.

Sometimes you get the things you desire, just not in the order you expected. That's why it's important to go after everything that you want, even if it doesn't fit your personal time line.

What to Do When the Timing Is Not Perfect

I have a friend who got pregnant very young. She had always known she wanted to be a mom, and was a naturally nurturing person who was great with children. However, because she wasn't in a solid relationship and was still in college, she didn't know how she was going to make everything work. She trusted her heart, and had already fallen in love with the tiny being that was growing inside her. She told her parents that she was going to be a mother. They agreed to help out, and she put her education on pause and had the baby. Later, when the child was a little older, she went back to school and graduated. She told me that it was not an easy road, and things didn't go exactly as she had imagined they would, but she had no regrets because everything she'd dreamed of happened, just in a different order. An added bonus to this unexpected change of plans is that she and her daughter are extra close because they grew up together, and to this day, the two continue to support and help each other.

From Your Past, But Don't Let It Hold You Back

Some children grow up in the worst possible circumstances, never knowing what it's like to be part of an intact, loving, family. Some wind up in the foster care system. That's what happened to one man who came through to me in a reading. While some foster homes are wonderful, the boy was unlucky enough to be bounced from home to home, and none of his experiences were good. He did get lucky in that he grew up, got out of the foster care system, and met a wonderful girl. They married, but because of his own horrible childhood he was afraid to have children. His wife wanted children, but she understood his fears. She gave up her dream of having her own family, did her best to be a wonderful aunt to her nieces and nephews, and became like a mom to all the kids in the neighborhood. Time passed, and the man eventually died.

His wife came to one of my events, and sure enough, her husband came through in a reading. He was desperate to tell her that he had made a terrible mistake. Looking back over his life, he realized that instead of worrying that his lack of parental role models would make him a bad father, he could have broken the cycle by having his own child and giving it all the love he himself had lacked growing up.

During his life review, he realized he'd let his own fears hold him back. He had loved his wife deeply, and was as capable of being a good father as he was of being a loving husband. He was so remorseful that he had robbed her of the chance to be a mother. He remembered how loving she was to the children in her life, and would have done anything to have gone back in time and changed things. Of course, it was too late, and he was destined to regret the chance he was so afraid to take.

This is a perfect example of how the fears from your past can affect your future. Spirit wants you to know that you always have the power to change your future, every single day that you are alive.

———

Taking the Leap

Alexa and I knew we wanted to have our first baby when we were still young. Our plan is to have three children, so we wanted to get started as soon as possible. We were surprised when our family and friends weighed in on that decision. A lot of people feel as if they have to have everything all set up before they bring a baby into the world. That means a house with a backyard, a big sport utility vehicle, and all the baby paraphernalia. We live in a nice condo, but as soon as Alexa got pregnant, the comments started. Everyone wanted to know when we were moving! "You are going to need a backyard, and space for the baby to play." This newborn baby wasn't even born yet, and friends and family were already worrying about where he was going to ride a bike and play ball! People were acting like we were going to raise Royce in a tent on the side of the road. I got a little freaked out, but then I thought about all the people raising kids in tiny apartments in New York City, or poor countries where the whole family might share a single bedroom. If people in those areas waited until every child could have their own room, a backyard, and a swimming pool, they'd never have children. I've learned from Spirit that when it comes to having children, as long as there is love, you don't have to worry about setting the stage perfectly—just let the show begin!

Infertility Doesn't Have to Be the End of Your Dream.

Some people want children and, no matter how hard they try, are unable to have their own biological offspring. Of course, they are not destined to live with regrets, and they usually come up with other ways to share their love. They may adopt a child or take in foster children. They might become nannies or teachers, or be extra close to nieces and nephews or godchildren. There's more than one way to be a parent or a nurturing figure in the life of a child. It's just when you put your life on hold and don't consider any alternative that you might find yourself regretting your decision.

I once had a client who struggled with infertility for years. She was never able to have kids, but she always felt her calling was to be a mother and have children of her own. For years, she felt like God had set her up to fail. She had no husband and no kids, and felt so alone, until one day everything changed . . .

She met a man at church who had lost his wife. They started seeing each other, and after a while, he introduced her to his children. They got married and suddenly her life turned around. She went from being lonely and alone to having a husband and three beautiful adopted kids who needed her love after their mom's passing. She understood that being a part of this family was her destiny. Not only did the children get a second mom, but she inherited a family.

Regret #2: Letting Your Soul Mate Slip Away

Family is going to be a major theme of this chapter, because when it comes right down to it, most of the enduring happiness and fulfillment you experience in life comes from the relationships you have with your children, spouse, and extended family. Unfortunately some people make mistakes when it comes to finding the person they will spend their life with. They might settle for someone they don't love out of fear of being alone. They may marry for money, or looks, and anything other than love. Some people find themselves in a comfortable relationship and never find the courage or motivation to find their true soul mate. They may not even admit to themselves that something is missing until their life review.

When "Mr. Right Now" Isn't "Mr. Right"

I did a reading for a woman, and her mother came through. She kept on talking about a man her daughter was involved with. The daughter insisted, "I'm not in a relationship!" The truth was that even though she didn't consider herself in a committed relationship, she had been dating one man for years. He checked all the boxes, and was good company, but she never felt true love for him. She knew he wasn't her soul mate, but she also knew that because she had never given him her heart, he could never hurt her. Her mother was desperate to communicate that the relationship actually was hurting her daughter!

Spending time with this man kept her "off the market" with no chance of finding real love. Her mother urged me to tell her daughter that she had to let him go, and she finally agreed. If the reading hadn't opened her eyes, this could have been a major regret! Instead, she broke up with the man and they were both able to move on and find someone to love and start a family with.

Sometimes your soul mate won't be the person you expect. That's where you have to trust your guides and look out for signs. Remember, when it comes to recognizing your soul mate, the signs might be subtle. You're not going to see a flashing neon arrow pointing to the person. Instead, pay attention to how you feel when they're around you.

I remember a friend of mine who had a wonderful connection with a co-worker. He was funny and kind, and they were best friends at work. He let her know that he wanted to take their friendship to the next level, but he was a few inches shorter than she was, and she worried that her friends wouldn't think he was as attractive as other men she'd dated. She insisted they had to stay "just friends." Then one day she learned that he had asked another woman out on a date. Suddenly her suppressed feelings rushed to the surface, and she realized he was the one she wanted to share her life with! Fortunately she let him know in time, he canceled his date, and now they're happily married with two wonderful children. Recently she commented how grateful she was that she hadn't let superficial concerns about his height and looks keep her from opening her heart to this amazing man.

Fear is often your worst enemy when you're trying to live your best life. You might be afraid to start a new relationship because of your own childhood pain over your parents' divorce or a difficult breakup you experienced. You might feel insecure or unlovable for a number of reasons, and be afraid to put yourself out there and take a chance at getting hurt. But the risk is worth it, and you have to push through the pain in order to open yourself up to love.

That doesn't just apply to relationships. People also let fear stand in the way of pursuing their dreams and goals, which leads us to the third common regret.

Regret #3: Not Pursuing Your Passion

If your Sunday afternoons are ruined by the thought that you have to go back to work the next day, or if time seems to stand still when you're in the office, chances are you're not in the right job. As a child, you probably had dreams of what you wanted to be when you "grew up." Along the way, you might have gotten discouraged and decided to settle for something practical, safe, and secure. Maybe you chose to please your parents and go into the family business, or listened to the advice of a counselor or teacher who barely knew you. There's nothing wrong with having a practical job or making your parents happy with your career choice—unless it robs you of your own happiness.

That's why it's important to check in with yourself when it comes to your work. Ask yourself if the job you're in is aligned with your interests, your passion, and your soul. If not, it's time to make a move—or risk looking back with regret.

You only have one life, so follow your passion.

Years ago, I had a woman come in for a reading who hoped to connect with her father. I immediately noticed that she seemed very nervous. I asked her what was wrong and she confessed that she was afraid of what her father would say when she told him she was going to sell the business he had worked so hard to build. It turned out, she had nothing to worry about. Her dad came through and instead of criticizing her choice, he said, "Good for you! I let my work consume too much of my time and keep me from my family. I want you to take the money and live your life differently than

I did." He told her that even though he was proud of the successful business he had created, when he was on his deathbed he had major regrets about how much of his life it had consumed. There were places he had dreamed of visiting with his wife and children, and important events he'd missed out on because he was so tied to his business. He didn't want her to have the same regrets. She sold the multimillion-dollar business, traveled, and eventually became a successful interior designer. She knew she wouldn't make the same amount of money as her father had, and it didn't matter to her. Living her best life meant infinitely more—and having her dad's approval confirmed that she'd made the right choice.

If you don't try, your odds of success are zero.

My dad's friend Pete was a basketball coach at an elite private school. He recently told us about a coaching seminar he attended. The person running the seminar shared a graphic that showed all of the schools that had basketball programs, and how many players participated. He explained, "There are millions of children playing basketball, and many of them dream of going pro, but out of all those players, only a small percentage will stick with it and go on to play college ball. Then, just a tiny percentage of those college players will make it to the pros." He wanted the coaches to realize that the odds of any of their players making the pros were stacked against them. But Pete had another perspective. He felt that even though it was a long shot, every year, new players were recruited to play professional ball. "Someone has to make the pros, and if there's a talented player on my team, I'm going to encourage them to try their best. The odds might be against them, but if they don't try, the odds are zero!"

Regret #4: Cutting People from Your Life
and Refusing to Forgive

A common theme that comes up again and again during readings is forgiveness. Holding a grudge against someone you love hurts everyone involved, and that fact becomes crystal clear during the life review.

Souls who refused to get over a grudge or heal a rift when they were alive are passionate about keeping their loved ones on earth from making the same mistake. That's why it's so common for a parent who has died to come through in a reading and beg their child to reach out to a sibling. It causes parents so much pain when they realize that their children are fighting, rather than supporting one another in their grief.

There are lots of reasons people choose to distance themselves from people they care about. Here are just a few of them:

> › They don't want to admit they were wrong after a disagreement, so they stay away out of embarrassment or stubbornness.

> › They're afraid of the other person not accepting their apology, especially if a long time has passed since they spoke or spent time together.

> › They want to be right so badly that they build a case against the other person, and keep adding evidence until they are unable to see the situation for what it is.

> › They're afraid or threatened by someone, so they cut them out of their life.

> They're in the habit of not taking responsibility for their actions, and instead have a pattern of walking away after a conflict—and never coming back.

> They prioritize material things and money over relationships.

> They take things too personally, and refuse to see the other person's perspective.

You Can't Fire Me, Because I Quit!

Fear of abandonment is a big reason that people push others away. People with this fear would rather cut someone out of their lives than run the risk of that person leaving them. They're afraid to be intimate, because they don't want to be hurt. Often they won't admit to themselves or anyone else what's really going on. Instead, they'll play the victim, wondering why they can't find someone worth staying with. What they don't realize is that they, themselves, are the common denominator. The habit of being the first to leave when the going gets rough keeps them from sustaining long friendships and relationships. Once again, fear and insecurity create a behavior that ultimately ends in the soul seeing the error of their ways in their life review, and deeply regretting their actions.

Controlling From the Grave.

When someone loses their spouse, they often worry that their dearly departed is looking down on them and judging their behavior. That's especially true when the surviving spouse starts dating again. What they don't realize is that no matter how jealous and possessive their husband or wife might have been in life, they leave those destructive traits behind when they enter heaven. When they pass, their only wish is that their loved one is happy until they can be reunited in heaven.

Before they die, however, some people do everything they can to influence their spouse and children. I've shared countless messages of apology from souls who attempted to put trusts and wills in place in order to control their loved ones from the grave. They might have left a child out of their will, leaving a legacy of pain and resentment. One husband left his wife all of his worldly possessions under the condition that she never marry again. Once he died, he wished he had done things differently, but it was too late.

Forgiving Is a Gift You Give Yourself

I want you to understand that I'm not telling you to be a pushover, condone bad behavior, or spend time with someone who is abusive or destructive. But letting go and refusing to let that person's actions cast a shadow over you allows you to move on.

The easiest way to avoid having regret over keeping a grudge, or cutting someone out of your life, is to understand that forgiveness is something you do for yourself. Holding in anger and resentment hurts you in the long run, in life and in death.

Letting Bygones Be Bygones

There are two times when you have to let go—and that's at weddings and funerals. Even if it means sitting at the table next to someone you've been feuding with for years, you owe it to yourself and everyone there to be the bigger person, and be polite.

I know a woman who cared for her ex-spouse when he became ill—even though the two had been divorced for years. They were still connected through their children, and she couldn't abandon him when he had no one else. She told me that she never regretted being the bigger person and being kind, and her children never forgot how she put the past aside and took care of their father.

Regret #5: Self-Sabotaging Behavior

We all want to live our best lives, but some people get stuck in destructive patterns that stay with them until the day they die. They might be addicted to drugs or alcohol, cheat on their spouses, or gamble away their life savings. They might let their own egos sabotage their careers or relationships. Or they might be greedy and unethical, and cause others personal and financial harm. You might wonder how these people get into heaven at all. The truth is, when they go through their life review, most of them see the error of their ways and are truly sorry. But being sorry isn't enough—which is why they spend their time in heaven helping others to overcome addiction and other negative behaviors.

Hitting the "reset button" in heaven.

People often think that if you find your soul mate, it's clear sailing from there. But just because you have found your soul mate doesn't mean you'll stay together. A lot can go wrong in life! I did a reading for a young woman who told me that her parents had met in high school, and they were happy together for years. The husband loved his wife, but a few years into his marriage he cheated on her. For fifteen years, they didn't speak. Then they both passed away a few years apart. Much to their daughter's shock, during my mediumship event, they came through to her together. The husband was truly remorseful, and his wife saw how much he regretted his actions. They were true soul mates, so they were able to forgive each other and were reunited in heaven.

The One Regret No Soul Ever Shares

Are you ready for this? In life, you might think that the house you live in, the car you drive, and how much money you have in the bank are measures of your success. Sure, that kind of thing matters on earth, but when you die, it's meaningless. In my years as a medium, no soul has ever come back to me and said anything about not having enough money. It's like the old saying: no one on their deathbed regrets not spending more time at the office. No one in heaven worries about the money or possessions they left behind.

When you look back over your life from a heavenly vantage point, here are some more things you won't regret:

› Loving your friends and family.

› Being the bigger person when there's a disagreement or conflict.

› Being kind to an ex for the sake of the children.

› Letting go of a grudge.

› Listening to someone and trying to understand their perspective.

› Helping someone when they really need you.

Sometimes in life, we are faced with things that are hard and emotional, but we have to go through them. Divorce, loss, conflict, and facing our fears are not easy to navigate, but the discomfort they cause is called *healing pain*. Healing pain has a silver lining, because it's what you feel when you're on the verge of a breakthrough. Facing the pain helps you to grow. It's when you try to avoid pain and let fear run your life that you wind up with regrets.

SPIRITUAL PRACTICE

WHAT SPIRIT WANTS YOU TO KNOW

Fear is one of the most common reasons people don't fulfill their destiny in life and wind up with regrets. A type of fear that we don't think about a lot is the fear of letting go. But it's really important to souls in heaven, because being afraid to move on from what's comfortable is something they see a lot—and souls often work through me to encourage the people they love to take a leap of faith.

Life can be like learning to do tricks on a trapeze! I know that there are places where you can do this, and it sounds fun—but also kind of scary! You swing for a while, but there's a point where you have to let go to grab the next trapeze in order to fly. It's not easy at first, because you have to trust that the next trapeze will be there and have the skill to be able to swing confidently along, grabbing on to each bar. You have to be brave (and it helps that there's a safety harness and a net!).

Just like letting go of the bar on a trapeze in order to grab the next one, when you let go and distance yourself from people who no longer serve you, you clear the path for more positive people to enter, and set yourself up for new adventures and experiences. Life is all about change, connection, and growth. You have to keep moving to get the most out of it.

Of course, the trapeze analogy only goes so far. Some people and relationships are meant to be with you through your whole journey of life, but others are just there for a period of time. Your spirit team, and your own intuition, will often nudge and guide you toward understanding the difference between the two.

Exercise: For Fewer Regrets, Tackle Your Bucket List Early!

We've all seen the movies where someone gets a diagnosis and realizes their time on this earth is limited. Suddenly they look at their life and realize there are things they need to do and places they want to see so they don't die with regrets. Guess what? You don't need a death sentence to be motivated to address these issues now! Grab your journal and consider some of these questions to help minimize regrets and lost opportunities, starting now.

JOURNAL PROMPTS

› What priorities do you need to set to ensure you don't regret not spending time on the things that are most important to you?

› If you can't figure out where your passion lies, journal about what you would do with your life if you were certain you couldn't fail.

› Write down goals you had when you were young that you've abandoned—or even forgotten about.

› Is there a place in the world that you've never been to, and would regret not seeing?

› Last but certainly not least, is there a relationship you
would like to heal or a person you need to forgive?
Write down some ideas for connecting to that person,
and think about what you would say to them.

As you respond to these prompts and compose your "No Regrets
Bucket List," remember that you don't have to limit yourself to one thing.
You can move forward on more than one area of your life at a time, so if
something is stalled, you can make progress in another area. Life isn't a
straight line—your existence can be as full as you want it to be.

Chapter 6

WAKE-UP CALLS

No matter how carefully you plan your journey through life, you're bound to encounter challenges and detours along the way. Your focus may drift, causing opportunities to pass you by, or the risks you take may not deliver the desired results. At some point you'll probably lose a job or a relationship, or have an accident or a health scare. There might even be a time when you find yourself in a dark place, plagued by addiction, bad habits, mental illness, or negative behavior. None of these experiences are anything to be ashamed or afraid of. After all, life is hard and unpredictable, and we're all just mortal, flawed human beings. That's why you're assigned a spirit team to help you through the hard times and sound the alarm when you need a wake-up call. Your guides nudge, push, and try their best to keep you on course, while your angels protect you both physically and emotionally, and your loved ones in heaven send you signs and signals, along with their loving energy.

Of course, your spirit team can try to influence and intervene when needed, but ultimately the life you lead is up to you. You can only hope that in the end you will have accomplished what you set out to do, learned some lessons, and spread some love and kindness, leaving a positive result to others.

SOMETIMES YOU NEED A WAKE-UP CALL

If you expect to make progress toward your goals and be your very best every single day, you're probably expecting too much from yourself. You don't need to be perfect, but you also don't want to ignore what's going on until things get out of hand. Here's what I mean. Imagine that your doctor advises you to lose weight because your blood pressure and cholesterol are high. You vow to change your ways and start eating healthy and exercising, and for the most part you keep that promise. If you're doing your best and sticking to your plan, you shouldn't beat yourself up for indulging once in a while. Skipping the gym or indulging in dessert or a cheeseburger occasionally won't undo all of your efforts. If you feel healthy and energetic and the numbers on the scale are moving in the right direction, you don't have anything to worry about. On the other hand, if one unhealthy choice leads to another and ignoring your doctor's advice becomes a habit, you run the risk of getting a dramatic wake-up call in the form of a heart attack or some other major medical event. While no one wants a major health scare, it sometimes takes something drastic to make you sit up and take notice.

Warnings and Signs Keep You Safe
and Moving in the Right Direction

A wake-up call is a warning that you're heading into destructive or unsafe territory. You probably experience some small, commonplace ones every day, like when you get in your car and hear the seat belt chime as a reminder to buckle up. In fact, cars have all kinds of warning signs, and the more sophisticated ones do a great job serving as a safety reminder if you're willing to pay attention and listen. I mentioned earlier in the book that your guides are like your GPS system in your car, helping you navigate your path. The rest of your spirit team also work together (like the safety systems in your car) to alert you to potential danger, suggest alternative routes and solutions, and call for help when it's required.

Pull Over and Rest!

Speaking of cars with warning systems, a friend of mine recently bought a new car with a very sophisticated system of sensors and safety features. She was coming to the end of a long drive late one night, and was very tired. She turned up the radio, opened her window, and did everything she could to stay alert for those last few miles, but it was no use. She actually nodded off for a second and jolted awake just as she was drifting into the next lane. Luckily there weren't a lot of cars on the road at that hour, and she was able to quickly swerve back into her lane. Her car sensors registered what was happening and the car began urging her to pull over. An outline of a coffee cup flashed on her dashboard with the words "Pull Over and Rest." The car was giving her an electronic wake-up call for her safety and the safety of others on the road. "I couldn't believe my car was telling me to get a cup of coffee," she told me the next day. She took the advice and pulled over at a Starbucks before getting back on the road to complete the remainder of her journey home.

Ignoring that sign could have been devastating, and she knew it. As she was sharing the story, I thought of the many wake-up calls we receive throughout the course of our lives. Some are physical and commonplace, like smoke alarms and car sensors. Others come from friends, doctors, and therapists, while the most significant often come from a divine source.

Here are a couple of examples of how divine intervention can deliver a subtle warning and keep you safe.

› You're driving your car and are about to turn into another lane. You've checked over your shoulder and looked in your rearview mirror, but suddenly you have a sense that there's something there—it's almost like something is holding on to your steering wheel. You look over your shoulder again and realize you've narrowly avoided a collision.

› You have an uneasy feeling about an area, like an elevator or parking lot, even though it's familiar to you. You trust your intuition and take another route, and later learn that someone was robbed in that area at that same day and time!

› Something tells you to steer clear of a new acquaintance. You later learn more about them, which confirms that your instinct was 100 percent correct!

WHAT IS UNIVERSAL KNOWLEDGE?

People sometimes question a message that comes through in a reading because they can't imagine how their loved one would have access to the information they're sharing—or even understand it. The explanation is always the same. Universal knowledge is like heaven's version of the internet, where an infinite amount of information is available—but in this case there's no need to google anything! Everything a soul needs to know about any topic is right there, instantly accessible as part of an awareness shared by all beings who have passed over since the universe began.

If it's difficult to get your head around this, it's no wonder. You don't have access to universal knowledge while you're alive, and it's hard to imagine what it would be like. I remember doing a reading for a stockbroker who was going through a lawsuit. His mom, who had passed a few years earlier, came through with some very sophisticated financial advice for him. "That's not my mom!" he burst out. "My dad did everything when it came to money—my mother didn't even have a bank account." I had a hard time convincing him that his deceased mother was actually not speaking from her own life experience, but instead was accessing the database of universal knowledge that's available to all souls in heaven. It's for that reason our loved ones in spirit can come through with advice for any topic or challenge our life brings. They always know how to guide us or help us because they are tapping into universal knowledge.

You're Not the Only One Who Learns
from Your Mistakes

Your loved ones, guides, and angels never judge you when you make mistakes. That's partially because making mistakes helps you grow and evolve as you travel through life, and also because you're gathering experiential knowledge that all souls will share when you pass over.

So what happens when you resist learning from your mistakes and keep making the same one over and over? When that happens, you might need a wake-up call.

Near-Death Experiences Are
the Ultimate Wake-Up Call

A near-death experience, or NDE, is when you actually die in this world and come back to life, defying medical odds. Usually this happens while you're at the hospital or in an ambulance. You stop breathing and are declared medically dead until the moment when you are miraculously brought back to life.

What's really happening here? When people are looking at your body and all signs of life are gone, what's actually happening at a soul level?

I've had the chance to talk to many people who had near-death experiences. Many of their stories are surprisingly similar: They saw a tunnel of white light and became aware of their soul rising up and out of their body. Looking down, they could see the doctors and nurses working on them and were also aware of familiar souls gathered around. They recognized loved ones who had passed over, along with their angels and guides. They immediately entered their life review and could see the meaning of their life begin to take form—but the review was cut short by friends and family in heaven telling them they had to go back. Many shared the feeling that they were brought back to earth with a mission or a specific purpose.

I've seen many people change after a near-death experience. It's like Charles Dickens's famous story *A Christmas Carol*, where Ebenezer Scrooge sees his life with a whole new perspective after he's visited by three spirits. Dickens's famous wake-up call transformed Scrooge from a miser who was greedy, insensitive, and money-grubbing to a loving and generous man who found the joy and happiness that had previously eluded him by connecting with and helping others. The same happens in real life with an NDE.

REAL-LIFE EXAMPLES OF
NEAR-DEATH EXPERIENCES

I've seen near-death experiences result in some amazing real-life transformations. Sometimes I don't see the evidence until the person has passed over for the final time!

Recently, in a reading, I brought through a father who had been an abusive alcoholic before having a near-death experience. He came back determined to make amends to all the people he'd hurt. He gave up all his addictions and vices and spent the next five years of his life getting to know his children. Although his remaining years were cut short, he made them count. Thanks to his wake-up call, he dedicated himself to making up for the time he'd lost due to alcoholism. In the reading, he stressed how lucky he felt to have received a second chance, and how precious that time had been to him and his family.

A man shared a near-death experience that occurred when he was having a routine appendectomy. There was a freak complication, and he died on the table, but the doctors brought him back so quickly that his NDE was cut short. He saw the light, and the tunnel had barely started opening when he was pulled back. Although he did not get the full experience, what he did see was enough to motivate him to take life more seriously. He was convinced that he had been saved for a reason, so he became more religious, and spent time helping people less fortunate.

I knew a little girl who was hit by a car and was in a coma. The doctors said there was no hope of her regaining consciousness, but miraculously, she emerged from her coma and made a full recovery. Later, she remembered being in heaven with her grandparents, and others who had passed, including a young schoolmate who had died of cancer. She shared that, while in a comatose state, she was out of her body, playing video games with her friend, when suddenly the game stopped and the girl said, "It's time for you to go back. I'm staying here, but tell my parents I'm okay and that I love them." At that point she opened her eyes, saw her family gathered around her, and eventually picked up her life where she had left off. She made sure to tell her friend's parents about having spoken to their daughter, and relayed the loving message. She never forgot what had happened while she was in the coma, and told me that not only had life become more precious to her, but she had a whole new understanding of what happens when we die.

Should I Stay or Should I Go?

Near-death experiences are rare, and they don't always turn out the same way. In some cases, when you die, your soul finds itself at a crossroads. It may be sent back to live for a while longer, while sometimes it will keep going and join the other souls in heaven. You can't always have a choice, but in some instances there is an exit point. Exit points are when you get the opportunity to either come back or transition. You might assume that given the choice, anyone would choose life. After all, it's hard to think about leaving everything and everyone you know behind. But I have connected with many souls, especially those who knew they would be in pain or impaired in some way if they came back, who chose heaven.

I had a young child who came through at a mediumship event. She had died after being on life support for a few weeks after a terrible accident. There was no hope of her living a normal life, but her parents could not bring themselves to make the final decision to take her off life support. When the day came when they had to pull the plug, they arrived at the hospital to find that their daughter had already died. During the reading, she explained that she had been given a choice to pass over or stay in her coma, and chose heaven in order to relieve her parents of the pain and responsibility of pulling the plug.

Sometimes souls get the chance to come back briefly. They are destined to leave this world but get the chance to come back for a short time. I remember a reading I did where the soul who came through had suffered a catastrophic heart attack. He told me that when he got to heaven he had been given the opportunity to come back and say goodbye to his family. He knew he would never recover, but was willing to experience the pain to share some final words of love, and give his family closure.

When Your Near-Death Experience Isn't

A friend of mine was accidentally shot when a gun misfired. Thankfully she survived, but when she looked back on that period when the paramedics were working on her, she remembered seeing only blackness. Because of that, she became petrified that there was nothing after she died. I did a psychic reading for her, and could see that her soul had actually never left her body, even though she was convinced that she had died for a period of time.

Not all near-death experiences are the same. Not everyone whose heart temporarily stops beating dies spiritually, and on the other hand, people can have some vital signs, but their soul might still leave their body for a few moments. Sometimes the doctor is the one who brings you back, and sometimes it's more mysterious and can only be attributed to divine intervention. If you are lucky, a doctor can bring you back when your body is still viable, but sometimes heaven has the power to bring you back when all other hope is gone.

What Near-Death Experiences
(Your Own or Someone Else's)
Can Teach You

People are fascinated by the idea of near-death experiences. I have a theory about them. I think heaven lets a few people get a glimpse of the afterlife so they can come back and give us all a little bit of hope. Knowing that their time on earth is just one part of the soul's journey can even inspire others to turn their lives around. In that way, a near-death experience can actually be a wake-up call for more than one person. They realize there's so much more to their journey than the time on earth, and that the things they're worrying about don't matter much in the grand scheme of things. That's why they get the courage to change careers, or fix relationships, or finally stop their destructive behaviors. They realize they're been blessed with a second chance, and they have a new perspective on how to make the best use of the time they have left.

NEAR MISSES AND CLOSE CALLS

You don't need to die and have a near-death experience to get a wake-up call. A wake-up call can be just about anything that sends you a clear message. For many people, it's a near miss that makes them realize what they're risking by their unsafe behavior. For some, this is all it takes to turn their lives around.

---

*"I could have died!" When a Near Miss
Makes You Change Your Ways*

A near miss makes you realize how precious life is. You were never dead, and you don't transition, but the awareness that your life could have ended is a huge wake-up call.

Here are some examples of near misses and the effect they might have:

› You look down at your phone while driving and notice a text message. In the few seconds that your eyes are off the road, a car coming toward you swerves out of the way, narrowly avoiding a head-on collision. You pull over, shaken, and the other driver jumps out of their car and gives you an earful. While you're apologizing, all you can think of is how a head-on collision could have killed you both. The near miss makes you a more careful driver, and you make it a point to ignore your phone when you're on the road.

› A workplace injury requires you to take strong pain medication, and you find yourself becoming dependent on the pills. You keep taking more and more, until your wife comes home to find you overdosed on the floor. You come to in the emergency room feeling grateful to be alive, and vow to overcome your addiction.

› You strive every day to move up the corporate ladder, making work your whole world. Not only do your

117

relationships with family and friends suffer but
your health does too. You don't exercise, and heavy
restaurant meals with clients cause your blood pressure
to skyrocket. When you wind up in the hospital with
what the doctor calls a "mild cardiac event," you realize
it could have been much worse. You turn down your
next promotion, start putting your health and family
first, and begin to create balance in your life.

Close Calls Make You Realize
What You Might Have Lost

While a near miss causes your own life to flash before your eyes, a close
call may also give you a glimpse of something else you may have lost. After
a close call, you might become hyperaware that you almost destroyed or
ended something important. You think to yourself, *Thank God I didn't*
make that choice—I'll never take that chance again!

Heavenly intervention often comes in the form of an event that shines
a light on what you're risking. But like any intervention, your awareness
and resolve to do better can fade over time. It's easy to go back to your old
ways if you don't have self-discipline and a good support group.

Here are a few examples of how a close call could wake you up to the
consequences of your behavior:

> › After years of marriage, things have gotten a little stale
> and you consider cheating on your spouse. You come
> close, but back out at the last minute. Afterward, you
> realize you would have gotten caught, and are suddenly
> horrified at the thought of losing your family.

› Your friend encourages you to make a risky investment in the stock market, but you don't get your order to buy in on time. The next day the stock plummets, and you realize how much of your savings you would have lost.

› You almost drown as a child but instead of being afraid of the water, you take swim lessons. As an adult, you make sure that everyone in your family is water-safe.

Sometimes the main purpose of a close call is to teach you to trust your intuition and keep you on the path to leading a good life and being the best version of yourself.

USE YOUR INTUITION TO TUNE IN TO DIVINE GUIDANCE

A close call is just one of the ways divine intervention can guide and protect you. You might not experience a near-death experience, or even an actual event. Sometimes a message comes in the form of a dream. You wake up from a particularly vivid dream, relieved that it wasn't real. If you're tuned in to your guides and angels, you might realize that the dream was trying to tell you something, and you vow to do everything you can to make sure that dream doesn't come true.

Sometimes your angels will use any means they can to help you. I remember when my mother was having terrible back pain. It got so bad that we took her to the emergency room, and when they did the X-ray, there was nothing wrong with her back. However, the X-ray picked up a mass between her heart and her lung. She had no pain in her chest, and had no idea it was there! If she had not gone to the hospital that day, she might have died. Instead, emergency surgery allowed her to make a full recovery. Her back pain never returned. The mass was unrelated to her back pain, but that pain was what made her go to the hospital, and it saved her life. I have no doubt in my mind that that was not a coincidence, but divine intervention.

I heard of another example where the angels actually spoke up. A woman was jogging and fell on cobblestones in Rhode Island. Her fall knocked the wind out of her, and she got up, feeling very disoriented. She felt strange, but she gathered herself and got in the car. She went home and took a nap, only to be woken by a voice saying, *You have to get help*. She drove to her daughter's house and had a car accident on the way. When the ambulance came, they discovered she had a brain bleed—from the fall earlier, not the car accident. The combination of being woken from her sleep, and the ambulance arriving so quickly after her car accident, saved her life.

Here's another example of how being tuned in to your own intuition can save lives. A teenage boy who lived with his mom was struggling with severe depression. He was seeing a therapist and assured his mother that everything was going fine. Even though he kept telling her that the therapy was helping, she had a nagging sense that things were not good with him. She went into his room, looked around, and saw that his medication bottles were full and he hadn't been taking them. She intervened and got him the help he needed, and was sure that she had saved his life.

We're here on earth to learn lessons, but our journey doesn't stop when we die. We still have the chance during the life review to learn and make amends by helping others, which is one of the reasons your loved ones in heaven watch over you and take such an interest in keeping you safe!

How will you respond to a wake-up call?

Of course, all the warning signs in the world won't work if you ignore them. I remember doing a reading a few years ago. A man came through and told me, "I didn't have to die!" He had collapsed in the bathroom and his family begged him to go to the doctor. He was afraid of what the doctor would say, so he kept putting it off, saying, "I'll go on Friday." It was too late. He died on Thursday, because his fear and denial kept him from taking care of himself.

Some people have a health scare and react with fear. They don't want to face the facts, and they push the whole thing away and don't change. Fear can paralyze you, which is why you should try to react with love rather than fear. If you respond with love and think about the people around you, you might get inspired to change for them.

This Is Not a Drill!

You can also think of wake-up calls as "spiritual alarms," a way for your soul team to keep you safe and on track.

In school, the teachers always told us to treat fire and carbon monoxide drills as the real thing. I remember one time, two students hid in the bathroom during what they thought was just a carbon monoxide drill because they thought it was cool, but there actually was carbon monoxide in the building. They wound up being okay, but if the windows in the bathroom had not been open, they could have been poisoned or even killed.

Another woman I knew was running up the stairs and clearly heard a voice in her head: *I shouldn't be doing this.* She was in a hurry and ignored it, and she fell and broke her leg.

BE YOUR OWN GUARDIAN ANGEL

When we go to heaven we bring the lessons and knowledge we've gathered and they become part of the bank of universal knowledge. But you don't have to wait! You can start sharing and receiving information right now. In the same way that spirits learn from other spirits, we can learn from the people around us. When someone is going through a divorce, think about the warning signs and what may have caused their problems. Use your intuition to understand, so you can help them and also learn from their experience.

Life is never going to be perfect, and you're bound to make mistakes, so be grateful that you have your spirit team to help you stay on course. To make their job easier, ask for their advice and be mindful and open to what they have to say. Finally, remember that you don't have to be dead, or experience a near-death experience to learn, change, and evolve. Just having an awareness of how your actions could affect you and the people you care about will put you in a better position to self-correct, so you won't need a more drastic wake-up call.

SPIRITUAL PRACTICE

WHAT SPIRIT WANTS YOU TO KNOW

If you feel like "something saved you" from losing your life, family, a relationship, or anything that's important to you, don't gloss over it. Wake-up calls are sent from your guides and angels to show you when you're on the wrong path. If you hit a roadblock, or narrowly avoid disaster, it might be a spirit warning you—so take a minute to stop and reassess. Even though heaven may have intervened once, you have free will, and are in control of your destiny, and it's up to you to get yourself on track.

*Try this exercise to reinforce what you've
learned about wake-up calls.*

Think of the most important people in your life and the lessons they taught you. Rather than trying to recall their words, focus on their actions and the example they set for you. Write down their names, the behaviors you observed, and how they influenced you then. Ask yourself, are you a different person today because of them?

For example, if your stepfather was an alcoholic, he might have taught you how addiction can make you lose the people you love. Years later, because of those memories, you might avoid overindulging in alcohol, and be more aware of how your actions impact your family.

Chapter 7

FULFILLING YOUR LIFE'S PURPOSE
(WHY DOES IT MATTER?)

One of the things I enjoy about being a psychic medium is that I have a "window" through which I can glimpse what happens in heaven. I'm able to learn how souls feel when they transition and go through their life review, and understand what motivates them to take on the task of helping people on earth. Because of my gift, I have access to this valuable information without having to experience death firsthand.

I feel so blessed to have been born with the ability to connect with the dead, and this book is my way of paying it forward by sharing the priceless knowledge I've received from souls on the other side. My hope is that you will benefit from their experience as much as I have. Remember that the wisdom I provide here does not come from me, but through me. With that in mind, the most important piece of advice I can relay is that you don't have to "wait till you're dead" to focus on the areas of life that matter most. When souls share their life experiences with me, what they treasure most are the relationships and loving memories. When you get to heaven, money and material things no longer matter. If you spend too much energy on your worldly goals, you run the risk of dying before completing your true destiny, or mission, on earth. And what happens then?

WHY FULFILLING YOUR DESTINY MATTERS

I've already told you that human beings are sent to earth to learn lessons and fulfill a predetermined purpose, but you might have a few questions about the details. You might wonder why it's important to accomplish so much in a relatively short lifetime? Aside from contributing to the vast database of universal knowledge, why does it matter that your soul experiences hardship and overcomes obstacles? And once you die, is the opportunity to learn and make a difference over? Do you still have a purpose when you get to heaven?

My intention is to help you understand enough about what takes place in the life review that you live your life with that in the back of your mind. I'm not saying you should be preoccupied with dying, but I hope that by pulling back the curtain on what happens in the afterlife, I'll inspire you to live your life in such a way that when your time comes, you can look back and know your soul accomplished what it was sent here to do.

And one more thing! In case you don't get everything done while you're alive, you can rest easy knowing you'll have the opportunity to continue your mission or make up for your regrets in the afterlife.

Your Life Review Isn't the End . . .

Going through your life review isn't like being in school and waiting to see if you received a passing or failing grade on your final exam. In that case, unless you have a very understanding teacher, your final grade is just that—final. After your work is evaluated and the results recorded, there's not much you can do to change it.

Fortunately life and the afterlife aren't like that. When you transition to heaven, your physical existence may be over, but you still have the chance to continue to do the things you love, and even make amends for any mistakes or missed opportunities that occurred when you were alive.

Because your soul is infinite, your life review isn't the end, it's the beginning! As you look back from your heavenly vantage point, you will clearly see the impact that you made during your time on earth. You'll revisit your decisions, good and bad, the people you helped and hurt, the important tasks you left undone, and have a chance to make things right.

You might come to heaven already knowing what you need to do or it might not be until you complete your life review that you discover your ongoing purpose, the "job" you'll take on in the afterlife.

Do Souls Really Work in Heaven?

When a soul transitions to heaven, they are in a perfect position to pursue their highest purpose, especially if they died with unfinished business, guilt, or regrets. You might be surprised—even disappointed—at the very idea of working in heaven, so let me clarify that for you. Pursuing your purpose in the afterlife is very different from working a traditional job. Here's the explanation I have received from my conversations with souls in heaven. Imagine you have the ability to pursue your passion without any earthly concerns like paying bills, commuting to work in traffic, or navigating office politics. You are free to spend your time on deeply meaningful pursuits that not only bring you personal satisfaction but make a profound difference in the lives of others. Now, once you're on the other side, your idea of a meaningful pursuit might be different from what it was when you were alive, but suffice it to say that there are countless ways souls can contribute to the well-being of others, and the planet. That's heaven's version of work, and many souls are drawn to take advantage of the opportunity.

Divinely Qualified to Help and Guide

You already know that when a loved one passes, they stay involved in the lives of the people they left behind, protecting, helping, and guiding them behind the scenes as a part of their soul team. In fact, their assistance may also extend to strangers who are going through some of the challenges they themselves experienced in life.

Souls who have died and gone through their life review have a unique ability to be of service for many reasons. Here are the most important ones:

> They are selfless. The work they do is completely spiritual in nature. They're not looking for a raise, a bonus, or a promotion. Their goal is simply to help the living.

> They see things with total clarity. It's as if souls in heaven possess a special kind of telescope that allows them to view everything, and everyone, from all angles. They can completely understand the impact of various actions, not just on the person directly involved, but on the people around them.

› They have access to all universal knowledge. Forget about Google! Souls can tap into the ultimate database of wisdom compiled by every being who existed, since the beginning of time.

The role that heaven plays in our lives is mysterious, and the divine work souls perform is not always evident, at least not directly. While you're alive, you can't possibly grasp the full role that your deceased loved ones, guides, and angels play in your life. Even as a medium, I don't have a clear picture of how souls in heaven guide the living. I have gathered some individual hints and examples from readings, but I believe they're just the tip of the iceberg when it comes to all the ways that our spirit team helps, supports, and protects us. Like many things that we can't completely understand, having an open mind and heart, and inviting and welcoming help from your heavenly team can enhance your journey through life, help you fulfill your purpose, and ease your transition to the afterlife.

WHEN PASSION LIVES ON

I knew a woman who had been a prima ballerina. For years she danced on Broadway, and she looked forward to performing in *The Nutcracker* every holiday season. As she got older, the rigors of dancing took a physical toll on her, and she eventually was forced to hang up her toe shoes. Her body may have let her down, but her love and passion for dance never faded. She was not willing to leave the world of dance, so in her later years she made it her mission to train and mentor talented young dancers. She was very selective and didn't take on just anyone, but sought out dancers who had the same drive and passion that she herself had. Even if a new dancer didn't have the same level of talent that she had been blessed with, she was able to help them leverage their love and commitment to improve their art. She had enjoyed an amazing career, and her ability to understand her students was uncanny. She could intuitively tune in to the hearts and souls of promising young dancers and understand what it would take to get them to the next level. It was her greatest joy to see a young dancer onstage living the same dream that she herself had experienced in her younger days.

This dancer was able to fulfill her destiny in life, but her experience was similar to that of many souls who pass over. They know what it will take for others to fulfill their dreams, and will nudge them and put opportunities in their path to help them succeed.

Just Like Souls Have a Purpose in Life,
They Also Have One in Heaven

Have you ever thought about that one thing in life you would have done differently? Do you have regrets, and feel like it's too late to resolve them? It's never too late! If you missed your calling here on earth, or didn't pursue your passion in life, you might be called upon to help someone else find theirs in the afterlife. For example, if the dancer in my last example lacked the opportunity or confidence to mentor students while she was alive, she could have guided them from heaven.

Souls Aren't Looking for a Permanent Vacation

Sharing your passion is just one of the ways souls take on a new purpose. You've been reading about how the jobs in heaven are different from the jobs on earth. Heaven is the ultimate paradise, and you might imagine that if you had the opportunity, you'd just hang out, relax, maybe check in on your loved ones from time to time. Instead, souls on the other side often choose to take on divine assignments by helping out those in the physical world. Remember, earth is the classroom where, ideally, you learn all of your life lessons before making the transition into heaven, but that's not always easy to do. That's why, once they're in heaven, many souls take the opportunity to help those in this world who are faced with similar struggles that they themselves experienced.

For example, someone who passed because of an accidental drug overdose will often provide support and guidance to those in the physical world who are going through a similar situation, using their divine skills to protect them and put people in their path who can help. Many times those on the other side will subtly nudge friends, family members, and total strangers to join support groups like AA, by putting them on the path, or even orchestrating wake-up calls. Often, those people look back on the co-worker who noticed that they needed help and took them to a meeting, or a compassionate friend who staged an intervention at exactly the right time, as a life-changing lucky break. But coincidences just do not happen. Often they are a result of someone in heaven pulling the strings.

The departed may help open the eyes of the family whose son or daughter is abusing drugs without them knowing, or signal to friends or family members to bring their loved one to the hospital right when an illness starts, so they can recover quickly.

They do this in discreet ways, by sending the family and friends signs, visiting in dreams, or speaking to them through their intuition. They aren't looking for credit—quite the opposite! Their goal is to help others in the best, most selfless way possible.

HOW DO YOU GET A JOB IN HEAVEN?

There might not be Starbucks or Macy's or Apple Stores on the other side, but there are still countless important jobs to do, and you can rest easy knowing that the task you take on will be something you're uniquely qualified for based on your life experience.

There are plenty of ways to help. Because there is so much need for heavenly guidance and intervention on earth, souls never have to compete or "interview" for the jobs. While most are committed to watching over and helping their loved ones, some are also motivated to help total strangers. They might take on this job for a short time, or for eternity.

When you align with your life purpose in this world, you might continue it in the afterlife. For example, someone who was a schoolteacher, and loved helping children learn and grow, might continue that work in heaven.

Souls are matched up with jobs in many different ways and for a variety of reasons. Here are a few examples:

› A job might be assigned to someone who has a special affinity or expertise for something. For example, a doctor might be tasked with watching over inexperienced medical students to make sure they don't cause a patient harm.

› Someone who suffered or struggled with a particular challenge in life might take on the task of supporting others in the same position. A soul who was unable to overcome addiction might use their divine influence to steer addicts toward rehabilitation clinics or support groups.

› Some people are born into difficult circumstances that color their entire lives. A soul who spent their youth in foster care and was left with emotional or physical scars might gain purpose in the afterlife by watching over and protecting children going through the same experience.

› In heaven, souls often try to make up for what they didn't do in life. During their life review, they realize that dying doesn't mean they get off "scot-free." If someone abandoned their children or shirked their responsibilities in some way, they welcome the opportunity to make amends and make it right.

› Souls often align with people who need help that only they can provide. For example, because of their unique, selfless perspective, a soul might help their surviving spouse find a new companion, or a parent who adopted a child might help reunite that child with their birth parent or other family member.

› A soul might take on something as simple as helping the loved ones they left behind heal from grief by giving them a new project or purpose.

› Someone who was killed or died in mysterious circumstances might make it their mission to help solve the case of their own death, in order to help their loved ones get closure and justice.

WHO WILL YOU CALL UPON FOR HELP, NOW THAT YOUR LOVED ONE IS GONE?

A lot of times people will come to me and say, "I feel so lost without my dad; he was an accountant and always helped me with my finances," or, "My mom was my sounding board. I depended on her for advice about my husband and family. Who is going to be there for me now?"

Your loved ones who have passed over care about you just as much as they did when they were alive, and they have lots of ways to support you. While you can't just pick up the phone and call them, you can definitely feel their presence around you. If you pay attention and tune in to your intuition, you'll see the signs that they are there. Here's an example that proves my point:

A father and daughter had a jewelry business together. The father especially loved the design aspect of jewelry making. He derived great satisfaction from creating things that were important to people. One of his specialties was making charms to commemorate special events. His business had started as a kiosk in the mall, and after a while he opened a store, but after twenty-plus years his labor of love was barely breaking even.

Sadly the father passed away, and his daughter struggled to keep the business afloat. Then, out of the blue, the girl met a marketing person and he offered his help. Within a few weeks, business was booming!

The daughter came to me for a reading and wondered if her beloved father had been pulling some strings and helping her. Sure enough, he came through and made it clear that he had connected his daughter with the talented marketing person. He was delighted to see so many people enjoying his designs and, most of all, was happy that he was still able to keep working and helping his daughter from heaven.

Just like you might call upon angels and saints who have specialties, like Saint Francis of Assisi for help with a pet, or Saint Anthony to locate a lost item, you can always call upon loved ones in heaven who have a certain expertise. They're usually happy to help!

Sometimes you don't have to ask. For example, your mom might have watched you search for love when she was alive. When she passes over, she will do everything she can to put your soul mate in your path or help guide you through a difficult divorce.

SAINTS AND ANGELS

So far, in this chapter, we've focused on how souls continue their purpose and make amends or their actions when they transition to heaven, but we can't ignore the good work that other members of your "soul team" contribute. For example, there are numerous saints who are known to help the living in particular situations. They stepped into these roles because of what they did when they were alive. After death, they further aligned with their purpose by making it their specialty to help everyone and anyone who calls upon them with that need. In addition to saints, there are angels who never lived in the mortal world, but are known for the special ways that they support the living.

Here is just a sample of the most well-known angels and saints, and the good works they are known for. Let's start with the angels:

› Archangel Michael: This angel is like a bodyguard with wings. Best known for his protectiveness and courage, he is

called upon for help in times of fear and uncertainty, and
to shield people from negative energies.

› Archangel Gabriel: This angel is all about communication
and divine messages. Archangel Gabriel helps in delivering
important news, guidance, and inspiration. Whether it's
creative endeavors, parenting, or spiritual guidance, Gabriel
is the go-to angel.

› Archangel Raphael: Need some healing? Archangel
Raphael is associated with physical and emotional healing.
He's called upon to guide individuals toward wellness by
helping them find the right remedies and solutions.

› Archangel Uriel: When it comes to wisdom and
illumination, Archangel Uriel is the one to turn to.
He helps with gaining clarity, making wise decisions,
and finding solutions to problems through insightful
guidance.

› Archangel Chamuel: Known as the angel of love, Archangel
Chamuel helps with matters of the heart, relationships, and
self-love. Need to find love, mend a broken relationship, or
foster inner harmony? Call on Chamuel.

› Archangel Jophiel: This angel is all about beauty and
inspiration. Archangel Jophiel helps in seeing the beauty
in life, bringing positive perspectives, and assisting with
creative endeavors and artistic expression.

> Archangel Zadkiel: Archangel Zadkiel is associated with forgiveness, mercy, and emotional healing. Call upon Zadkiel to help release resentments, find forgiveness, and experience emotional liberation.

Many saints carry on the good work they did in life, after they die. Here are some of these:

> Saint Peter: The leader of Jesus's apostles, Saint Peter started out as a fisherman before becoming one of the first disciples. He played an important role in establishing the early Christian Church. He is the patron saint of fishermen and popes.

> Saint Thérèse of Lisieux: Often referred to as "The Little Flower," Saint Thérèse of Lisieux lived a simple life based around love and kindness. She is recognized for her "Little Way," which emphasized finding holiness in everyday acts of kindness and service. She is the patron saint of florists, foreign missions, people who have lost parents, priests, and the sick. People pray to her when they need help feeling God's love.

> Saint Rocco: As the patron saint of illness, his divine job is taking care of those suffering from contagious diseases. As you might expect, he was very busy during Covid, because so many people called upon him for help. At the time when he was alive, Italy was in the grip of an infectious illness, and Saint Rocco cured

many people through praying over them and making the sign of the cross.

› Saint Francis: He is the patron saint of the environment and animals. He loved all creatures and allegedly preached to dogs, cats, livestock, and birds. In recent years, many congregations have started to bless pets and other animals as a way to honor his spirit and keep his legacy alive.

If you look at the lives of the saints, you can understand why they have taken on their jobs in heaven. In the same way, if you give it some thought, you might be able to see and understand your own purpose in life and predict what your ongoing responsibilities might be in heaven.

LIFE EXPERIENCE NEEDED!

Sometimes it's not enough that someone has the training and knowledge to help you. If you're like me, you want the empathy and unique under-standing that only comes from direct experience. That's why souls can be so helpful to the living. They've not only experienced life, but have the perspective that comes from looking back and seeing the results of their actions.

Here's a real-life example of why experience matters. There was a young Realtor who tried to help Alexa and me buy a house. Although they had taken all of the required courses, and had helped others buy homes, they had never actually purchased and owned a home themselves. We worked with that Realtor for a while, but it just didn't give us the confidence we needed to take this step! We needed someone who had personally gone through the experience of buying their own home to help us. Even though we understood that our original Realtor could probably navigate the paperwork and lead us through the process, we wanted someone who understood the emotional side of the transaction. When we found that person, it gave us the confidence we needed to move forward.

Sometimes people will come back to do some very unique and specific jobs.

You have a purpose in life, and based on how you live your life, you get a new purpose in heaven.

A Guide for Guide Dogs

One soul I connected with during an event had been blind since birth and depended on his seeing-eye dog to get around safely. He had always been convinced that his dog was almost human, because it seemed to understand his words and pick up on his emotions even more than the people in his life. When the man passed over, he took on the job of working through other guide dogs to help them understand how to give their owners the kind of support he had gotten from his beloved dog. He was not reincarnated as a dog, but was able to help both guide dogs and their owners form a strong mutual bond so they could work together as effectively as he had with his own guide dog.

A LIFESAVING JOURNAL ENTRY

This reading illustrates how a soul in heaven helped his mother discover information that would ultimately keep his twin brother from succumbing to the same risky behavior that had caused his own death.

There were two twin brothers who both struggled with addiction, until one died from an overdose and passed away. The surviving twin couldn't imagine life without his brother. He was consumed by dark, suicidal thoughts. Over time, he became more and more overwhelmed by his addictions. He started writing in a journal, pouring all the thoughts he was having about ending his life onto the pages. His brother in spirit guided his mother to find the journal.

She had brought his laundry to his room and was tidying up when suddenly she got an uneasy feeling. She had a feeling he was hiding something. She felt bad about invading his privacy; however, the feeling was making her sick. Fearing that it was drugs, weapons, or something illegal, she discovered something much worse: the journal.

She immediately brought her son to a psychiatrist and got him the help he needed. His mother had been in so much pain about her son's passing that she was oblivious to the fact that her remaining son was at risk for the same fate his brother had succumbed to. It wasn't until she had the unusual compulsion to clean her son's room, and was guided to find the journal, that she became aware that he was in crisis.

A Dream Lives On

There was a man I read for whose father had died when he was an infant. The young dad had been an automobile mechanic, and he dreamed of opening an auto body shop of his own and working on cars. He never realized his dream because he died when his son was three months old, and the baby was raised by his mother and grandmother. When he grew up, the young man became as infatuated with cars as his father had been. He could change a tire and replace an oil filter at thirteen. In fact, any task having to do with cars came naturally to him. Later on, he opened his own body shop.

In our reading, it became clear that his dad had been with him all along. He was a mentor to his son from heaven, and helped the boy to realize the dream that they both shared.

SOULS CONTINUE TO SUPPORT THE THINGS THEY CARED ABOUT IN LIFE

There isn't a wall between life and the afterlife, and often someone's life's work doesn't end when they pass. I believe the same people who spend their lives on research in science and health are helping others today with their research. The work of the new team is built on the foundation of scientists that have passed over, and continue to be guided by the souls who started the work.

A woman in our community died battling breast cancer. Her family built a foundation. When her family worked to create this legacy, she worked from heaven to bring this to other people's consciousness.

SPIRITUAL PRACTICE

Exercise: The Rocking Chair Test

A friend of mine once told me about something called the rocking chair test. It's a simple visualization exercise to help you understand what truly matters at the end of life. To start, imagine that you are ninety years old and retired. Picture yourself rocking back and forth in your rocking chair. Ask yourself: What will you look back on? What moments of your life truly mattered most?

Think about what thoughts came to mind as you "rocked." Did you like what you saw? The person you have become?

What moments were most important to you?

Make a list of the treasured memories you hope to have—wonderful vacations with family and friends, joyous holiday celebrations, and important events like weddings, births, and graduations. Now think of your passions and gifts. What contributions are you most proud of? How do you hope to be remembered? Immerse yourself in the experience of looking back over your life. Is the ideal version of your life review realistic? How can you make changes now to ensure that your real memories and experiences match your expectations?

Journal about your experience.

The rocking chair test helps us to stay living in the present. Sometimes the things that feel so big and important right now will not pass the rocking chair test.

For example: Your car keeps breaking down and the mechanic can't seem to find the issue. You are angry after spending days and weeks without a car, having to fight with the mechanic and feeling like you are losing brain cells with all the stress it has caused you.

Fast-forward to the rocking chair test: When you are in that rocking chair at ninety, do you really think you will remember this situation—or even the car itself? Truth is that it will most likely just be a tiny blip in your mind. That tells you something important! If it doesn't pass the test, it doesn't need to weigh on your heart.

WHAT SPIRIT WANTS YOU TO KNOW

Take time now to refocus on the things that your future self will thank you for. Most of the time, the things that you think are so big and important right now might not matter in years to come. However, what does matter is that you stay on your path. Baby steps, although they seem small, add up and will lead you to the life you dreamed you would have. Time is not running out. Your time here on earth may be limited, but you have all of eternity to accomplish your true divine mission.

Chapter 8

GETTING YOUR TRUE SELF BACK

You might wonder why, even with angels, guides, and loved ones in heaven watching over us, we humans still experience illness, addiction, and injury in this world. While your spirit team does everything they can to make sure you fulfill your destiny and benefit from your time on earth, the fact remains that your physical mind and body are susceptible to things like Alzheimer's, cancer, alcoholism, and a host of other ailments. However, while your mental and physical health may be vulnerable, your soul remains untouched, and when you transition to heaven, you leave the effects of your earthly challenges behind and present yourself in your purest, most authentic form.

Often in readings, people who have lost a leg due to diabetes will appear to me walking and fully healed. Someone who wore false teeth when they were alive will show off a beautiful, natural smile in heaven. Perhaps my favorite thing to see is a person who was burdened with Alzheimer's or dementia who can suddenly recall everything, even things that they weren't aware of at the time, once they transition.

WHAT DO SOULS LOOK LIKE IN HEAVEN?

When you picture your loved one in heaven, what do you see? You might imagine them as they looked the last time you were together, but it's more likely that another image comes to mind. In fact, depending on how close you were and how much time you spent together, you might have a whole "slideshow" of memories of that person—and that's actually a pretty good way of describing how a soul presents itself in the afterlife.

People often ask me what souls look like when I connect with them, and there isn't a simple answer to that question. You have to understand that when a medium connects to Spirit, what comes through is on a different "frequency" that can be disjointed and difficult to decipher. With experience, I've learned to translate what I see and hear so that it makes sense to the person receiving the message. During a typical reading, I will receive a series of quick impressions of the soul I'm connecting with. I'll get a sense of how they presented themselves, and what they liked to wear. I'll be able to tell from their expression what their personality was like in life. Those images reflect the essence of the soul, rather than being specific to any particular age or point in time. That's because keeping track of your age and time is important when it comes to your earthly existence, but it has no place at all in heaven. When you transition to the other side, there are infinite versions of you!

The best way I can explain it is that when you die, your soul reflects every phase of your life, all at once.

WHICH IMAGE IS THE REAL YOU?

To get a feel for what that's like, take a look at your baby book or a photo album from your childhood. I'm the oldest child, and my mother was very dedicated to recording all the milestones of my life, big and small. She saved tons of photos of me as an infant, a toddler, and during every school year, from kindergarten to high school graduation. There are albums packed with memories from holidays, graduations, family trips, and other significant events. Every photo reflects a different version of me, and all of the images exist together on a shelf in my mother's living room. Is one of these photos the "real Matt"? No! They're all me. And the cool thing is, in the same way that many, many pictures of yourself can be stored in an album or online, different versions of yourself are stored in your soul.

YOUR SOUL'S DATA IS STORED "IN THE CLOUD"

A good analogy to understand how this works is to think about how all of your computer data is kept in the cloud, which is just a huge database on the internet. The same thing is happening with your soul. Just like in the digital cloud, your soul's "data" can't be lost or destroyed. You will change, grow, and age, and all the while continue to add to your soul's data base.

Recently I lost a file on my computer. I found out that there's a piece of software called Time Machine that lets you go back to any point in time and search through your computer. Time Machine actually re-creates your desktop and files just as they were at any particular point in time. It was kind of cool going back and seeing everything I was working on, and what was important to me—even the events that were on my calendar—during that time.

Your soul is the same way. When you go through your life review, you're able to see all of the stages of your existence. You can see your fluctuations in weight, along with the styles, trends, and phases you went through. You may have had big hair in the '80s, or been a punk rocker in 2000. All those snapshots in time are stored in your soul. However, there is one version of yourself that captures the essence of who you are. That's the image that comes through when I connect with a soul during a reading.

WHAT DOES YOUR AUTHENTIC SELF LOOK LIKE?

Chances are, if you think back on your life, you can pick out a time when you looked and behaved the most like your authentic self. It's probably the way those people who love you and really "get you" would describe you.

This happens a lot with celebrities. For example, when Tina Turner passed away, her illness had caused her to stop singing, dancing, and doing all the things we associated with that iconic performer. However, instead of the media and social networks sharing images of her as she appeared during her last moments, they shared her most iconic moments. Although age and illness may have changed her appearance over the years, in those final posts and tributes, we saw the vibrant, talented Tina we remembered!

I remember being on a talk show called *Red Table Talk: The Estefans* hosted by Gloria Estefan. When I had watched her on previous episodes of the show, Gloria had straight hair and a business suit. I have to admit, I preferred the woman I thought of as the "real Gloria," with her wild hair and cool style. But to my surprise, when I was scheduled to be interviewed on *Red Table Talk: The Estefans*, Gloria walked onto the soundstage wearing an embroidered kaftan with her hair in my favorite curly and natural style. I said, "Gloria, I love how you look!" and she said, "Yes, this outfit captures who I really am." We both recognized her true self and felt more comfortable with that version of her.

Every one of us has roles they have to play in life, but no matter how we have to dress for work, for sports, or to fit in with our friends and social group, within us is always our essence—which is reflected in our style, behavior, and all of the intangible things that make each one of us unique.

The same way that in today's world we put a lot of thought and effort into choosing our profile photo for social media, in heaven we present ourselves in the image that represents our best, most authentic version of ourselves.

When I started to notice how people showed up in heaven, it inspired me to do more teaching about this, because those things that are most meaningful to us in life become part of our identity at a soul level. It can be a bit confusing, because there are no brand names in heaven or designer clothing manufacturers. But although your shopping days end when you pass over, your true style will remain a part of you for all eternity.

WHY YOU WON'T SEE A DEATHBED PHOTO IN AN OBITUARY

Obituaries are a tribute to the life, relationships, and accomplishments of a person who has passed over. They will often lead with a wedding day photo or a military picture. My mom used to think that was weird, because those photos were often from decades earlier, but to me it made total sense. People seeing the obituary would connect with the person they had known, and might not even recognize a photo of the person at the end of their life. I might not have recognized Tina Turner from a photo taken at the end of her life, and I'll bet she wouldn't have wanted to be remembered that way.

Most of our loved ones wouldn't want to live on looking as they did in their weakest, most vulnerable days, which is why they choose how they will be represented and portrayed to others in the afterlife.

WHAT I SEE DURING A READING

During a reading, I often will get an impression of a spirit who is dressed up in their favorite outfit, looking as if they just stepped out of the hair salon. Even though they are no longer in their physical form, and definitely don't have to worry about styling their hair or choosing clothes, their true self is presented to me so I can share what I see and they can be recognized by the loved one who is receiving the reading.

Once, at a live show, a woman came through who was the epitome of Jacqueline Kennedy Onassis. She had it all! She was decked out in a bouffant hairdo, tweed suit, and big glasses. When I shared what I saw, her daughter was blown away! "That's my mom! Jackie was her style icon and she tried to be just like her." The woman went on to explain that as she got older, her mother had adopted a new, more modern style, but at her core, she still embraced her inner "Jackie O."

Everyone was impressed with my detailed reading and description of the woman's style—except for one audience member. As soon as the event was done, she took to social media, saying, "Matt, how dare you describe someone's clothes in heaven. Everyone is naked in heaven!" I almost spit out my coffee when I read her comment! In all my years as a medium, I have never seen a naked soul. Souls come through in uniforms, workout clothes, Sunday best, and even lingerie.

Inked for Eternity

One man came through in a reading and I saw that he was covered in colorful tattoos. I told his mom, "Your son is here and he's all tatted up. He's pointing to each one and telling me their meanings." The woman couldn't believe her son still had his tattoos in heaven, but she loved it. He had been a successful tattoo artist, known for the unique, beautiful designs he created for himself and others. While every tattoo doesn't last for an eternity, the designs he had adorned himself with were an essential part of who he was at the deepest level, and they remained a part of him even after he passed over.

"HEAVEN SCENTS"

Scent is another part of your identity that can linger after death. I can't tell you how often smells come through when I do a reading! Perfume, cigarettes, cigars, motor oil. Special scents that are associated with the person in life can often cling to their soul after they pass.

For example, I had an aunt who loved Dunkin' Donuts coffee. Her daily ritual was to walk over to her local Dunkin' Donuts to have a cup of coffee and a cruller, and read the paper. Because of her morning routine, she absorbed the mouthwatering smell into her very being, and always carried the trace of coffee and donuts. Now that she has passed over, she sometimes comes to me with a message for my mother or another family member—and when she does, I always smell the sweet, familiar scent I associated so strongly with her when she was alive.

THE "REAL" YOU?

Who determines what is part of your soul identity and what isn't? There are no "official" rules or guidelines to help you separate the two. Your authentic self is a very personal thing. That even goes for the alterations you might make to your natural body. You can change everything from your hair to your nose to your gender, and if those adjustments unlock the "real you," then you carry them with you to heaven. For example, I had heard that the iconic comedian Joan Rivers loved how her face looked after her plastic surgery. Sure enough, one day she came through to me in a reading looking like the enhanced Joan that we were familiar with from the *Tonight Show*. She did not revert to her original, natural face when she passed over. Why? The image she portrayed in heaven was the way she saw herself—her true essence!

Losing Your Soul's Identity

Remember how we talked about how everything that happens to you in life is stored in a spiritual database? Your memories are stored in two places—your brain and your soul. In your soul right now is every version of you in your life. Even the moments you may have forgotten, like taking your first steps or opening your eyes for the first time, your soul remembers. So when you transition on to heaven, everything comes back in great detail, and you return to the best version of yourself, without illness, addiction, or any of the negative things that we leave behind. By "best," I don't necessarily mean the prettiest version—but the one that is most authentically you.

Authenticity Isn't Always Pretty!

For example, I had a grandma come through with chin hairs. The family was laughing when I described an elderly woman with six or seven hairs sticking out of her chin. One person pointed out, "You'd think she would have trimmed those when she got to heaven!" But those hairs were such a part of her—everyone had joked about them when she was alive—that they remained with her, even in heaven.

WHY DO WE GET SICK?

People ask me all the time, why do we get sick? Like I said earlier in the chapter, you're human, and your physical body is vulnerable. But when it comes to your essence—or your soul—that's a whole different situation.

Imagine you are like a home. When you build a house in this world, you repair it and maintain it. But no matter how well you maintain it, you can't protect it from unforeseen storms or earthquakes or other catastrophes. That's why you take out insurance on your home, so if something happens, you can rebuild it back to the way it was. It's the same in heaven—you can build yourself back to the way you were before. Your home and your body are physical things, and they're vulnerable. You can do your best to maintain them, but in some cases that's not enough. But you can insure your home, and you can insure your soul by living your best life and making it to heaven.

Insurance Policy from Heaven

A woman lost her son, who had been born with a terrible illness. While he was alive, he couldn't speak or walk. It broke her mother's heart to see him suffer, and she would have done anything to see him run and play and be a happy, active kid. The boy died at thirteen, leaving his mother so angry with God. Then, after many years, the mother passed away and her daughter came to me for a reading. The mother came through and said, "When I was alive, I went through something horrible, and I was left wondering why God would do this to an innocent child, and to me! When I died, I was able to reunite with my boy and see him walk, talk, laugh, and run! If I'd only known that he'd be made whole and healthy in heaven, I wouldn't have hurt so bad when I lost him."

I'm not the only person who's seen someone who was sick or had dementia restored to their best version of themselves in spirit. You may have had a deceased loved one visit you in a dream, and noticed how young, healthy, and happy they seemed. Many people discount dreams like that, but they are a common way for your loved one to reach out to you. They love having the opportunity to show you their true self, free of all pain and sickness.

Because of illness, people sometimes can't comprehend things. I did a reading for a woman who had lost her mother. The elderly woman suffered from dementia and didn't know who she was. Her daughter decided to bring her mom to come and live with her. She thought being together would help her mom to remember, but it didn't work—in fact, one day the mother pointed to herself in the mirror and didn't even recognize herself. The poor daughter cried every day, because her mom didn't recognize her and didn't seem to understand how much she was doing for her. To her shock, when her mother died, she came through in a reading and wanted her daughter to know she was now aware of everything she had done for her. The woman was so relieved because she had unselfishly cared for her mom for years, and finally knew that at a soul level, her mom was aware and able to recall every moment and loving deed.

SPIRITUAL PRACTICE

WHAT SPIRIT WANTS YOU TO KNOW

You don't carry your pain and suffering, or even your age, with you when you cross over. If you lose your hair because of chemo or if you lose your teeth, you will be made whole in heaven. Illness is a physical thing; it doesn't reach you at a soul level. There's a pure, true part of you that will always endure. It's just like when your physical house burns down, but the memories of home are still there.

Exercise: Imagine Your Loved One in Heaven

Imagine that you are a medium, and you are talking to a loved one in heaven. Ask them how they look and feel today, and open yourself up to receive answers from them. Ask them how they would like to be remembered.

If you are haunted by memories of the person when they were sick and dying, have an honest dialogue with them about it, and ask them to help you replace those images with ones of them happy and whole.

One good way to visualize them as they are in heaven is to go back to your earliest memories of your time together. Try drawing a picture or journaling about the memories. You'll find that the act of writing helps you to channel the memories. In this exercise, you're acting as your own medium, and you might find writing helps you solidify your connection.

Chapter 9

EARTHBOUND SPIRITS:
TRAPPED BETWEEN TWO WORLDS

I often meet people who worry that a loved one didn't make it to heaven because of the way they lived. Sometimes they're afraid to get a reading because they don't want to find out that their dearly departed is stuck in a kind of limbo, between earth and heaven. They're usually surprised when I explain that it's very rare for someone not to cross over. The reason for this is that deep down, most people have good intentions and want to live a productive life.

Fortunately you don't have to be perfect to get into heaven. If you make mistakes, there are many opportunities to redeem yourself, both during your time on earth and in the afterlife. Even if you're not aware of some of the damage you have done, you can rest assured that everything will come to light during your life review.

When a soul goes through their life review, they have the chance to look over their past actions and gain clarity on their behavior. It's an eye-opening experience to see your words and deeds all laid out in front of you, and at that point, most souls become very motivated to set things right. They will often take on tasks in heaven that help others learn from their misdeeds. An addict might guide others to sobriety, a greedy, selfish person might influence others to be generous and giving, and a violent criminal might help others avoid a life of wrongdoing. By recognizing their past behavior and working to help others, they can make up for their shortcomings and earn their space in heaven.

BLOCKED FROM HEAVEN: HOW SOMEONE BECOMES AN EARTHBOUND SPIRIT

Not all souls are interested in redemption. While most welcome the opportunity to help others avoid the mistakes that they made in life, there are occasions when someone is truly evil and has no remorse for their actions and no desire whatsoever to set things right.

These are the souls who "fail" not only life, but their life review.

Unable to cross over into heaven, they are destined to remain stuck between heaven and earth as earthbound spirits.

Before I dive deeper into the topic of earthbound spirits, souls who have no remorse for their wrongdoings and are unable to successfully cross over to heaven, I want to talk about the reason they are so rare and clear up a couple of misconceptions about why someone might be refused entry into heaven. This knowledge will not only give you peace of mind, but might protect you from being taken advantage of by unscrupulous people who prey on the grief and concern of others.

People will often ask me to help their loved ones make it to heaven, but there's nothing I can do. It's between the soul and their God. But some psychics, mediums, or, more often, unethical people posing as psychics or mediums, will jump at the chance to get involved. I've had countless people tell me about people who have reached out to them on social media, offering to "help a loved one to cross over." Usually they want money. It's hard to imagine someone wanting to take advantage of a grieving person's desire to know that their loved one is safe and at peace. But here's one situation where that almost happened:

I met a woman who had lost her son and was having a very difficult time dealing with her grief. The two had shared a close relationship, and after he passed she was desperate to connect with him and make sure he was okay. Unfortunately, in her efforts to reach her son, she came across a medium who told her that her boy was stuck between two worlds because he could see how sad she was and didn't want to leave her alone. The "medium" wanted her to meet with him many more times, at considerable expense, so he could "help her boy transition to heaven." Because she was in such a vulnerable state, she believed him. Fortunately, before she got in too deep with the other medium, she came to one of my events and I was able to help her connect with her son. By relaying his messages to her, I was able to prove that he had, in fact, already transitioned to heaven, and was watching over her.

Hearing about this kind of thing really upsets me. I can't believe that anyone could be so unethical that they would take advantage of a grieving mother. Not to mention that what they were saying was 100 percent false! Not wanting to leave a loved one behind will never prevent a soul from successfully crossing over. As they transition from life to death, souls gain a whole new understanding, and quickly realize that they can still watch over their loved ones from the other side. In the situation I just shared, there would be no way that the love this son had for his mother, or her grief over losing him, would have kept him trapped between worlds. That's not how heaven works. It's the same thing when someone is murdered in this world. They don't get stuck between the two worlds until their murder is solved. They transition and watch over things from heaven. You don't have to "let a person go," and your grief will not prevent them from crossing over. Your loving will keep their memory alive and draw them near to you in spirit, but will not cause them any problems when they transition.

YOUR CONSCIENCE IS YOUR COMPASS

On the surface, being banned from entering heaven may seem like a legitimate concern for many people. Life is complicated and filled with opportunities to slip up and make mistakes. If you're like most of us, when you look back over your life you can think of a million situations where you could have done better. But here's the good news. The fact that you're having those thoughts and concerns tells me you have nothing to worry about! The reason you are questioning yourself is because you have a conscience, are aware of your behavior, and want to do the right thing. Listen to your heart, and let your conscience be the compass that guides you. And remember that you don't have to be perfect to be welcome in heaven. If you did, heaven would be empty!

EVERYONE MAKES MISTAKES—
ADMITTING THEM IS WHAT COUNTS

We are all human, and we make mistakes. When someone has remorse for something they've done, it tells me they're on the right path, and they can get "extra points" if they try to make amends for their mistakes while they're still alive. I remember being a child and going to church. The priest would talk about sin and, being so young, I'd worry that one bad deed would doom me for life—and beyond! Of course, as an adult (and someone who has a little extra insight about heaven and the afterlife), I know that every one of us is given many chances to make up for our actions. It just takes awareness and the desire to do the right thing to make it happen.

When You Do the Wrong Thing for an Understandable Reason

Sometimes people behave in negative ways because of severe grief, pain, or trauma. They may have been carrying their burden for years, with no way to release their bad feelings other than to lash out at others. Everyone knows someone who grew up in a dysfunctional family whose pain causes them to act out. You might label that person as unfortunate or damaged, but you wouldn't call them evil.

Some people act badly because of conditions that are not their fault. They may suffer from mental illness, addiction, PTSD, Alzheimer's, dementia, or some other condition that makes it difficult or impossible for them to control their behavior. Again, their situation doesn't make them evil, and they can look forward to being clearheaded and healthy in heaven. At that time, they'll be in a position to help others on earth struggling with the same challenges.

When You've Been Punished Enough in Life

You may have a crotchety neighbor who makes everyone on the street miserable, but that doesn't mean they will not make it into heaven. Even though they are an angry, unpleasant person, they are not evil. In fact, they are punishing themselves, because their behavior robs them of the joy and companionship they could experience by being loving and friendly.

Many people punish themselves for their actions more than God ever could:

> *I connected with a soul during a reading who had caused a car accident shortly after he got his driver's license at age sixteen. He was arrested, but because it was an accident and he was such a young and inexperienced driver, he was never charged. Even though he never went to jail, he was punished for his actions because after his trial, he became an outcast. His family disowned him, and he was the talk of the town—and not in a good way! He lived with years and years of guilt. He survived well into his eighties, but every day was haunted by the fact that he had killed this man. He never got over what he had done, and for his entire life, he suffered from panic attacks and nightmares. At random times he would find himself replaying the accident in his mind, and he would cry and grieve all over again. He was convinced that he would be barred from heaven, and would never transition to the afterlife.*
>
> *When he came through to me, he told me that when he died, he expected to be punished, but God knew he had already suffered every day of his life. He was given the opportunity to connect with the man he had killed in heaven, and tell him how sorry he was, which allowed him to finally heal.*

Some People Just Don't Know Any Better

You might even know someone who was born into a life of crime and never knew any other way of life. While they could choose to take a different path, they tend to stick with the life they are most familiar with. When they pass over, they will be held accountable for their actions, but will have the chance to redeem themselves if they show remorse and make amends.

My great-uncle was in the mob, and committed every sin you could think of, short of actually killing someone. He was fully aware of what he was doing, and was motivated by money and lacked compassion for other people. He went to jail many times during his life, but every time he was released, he'd go right back to his old ways. His explanation was that it was the only life he'd ever known. There are many reasons why people in the mob can't get out, and in his case it might have been fear of repercussions, or just habit, but he never changed his ways.

When he passed away, he never transitioned to the other side. My mom, being a medium herself, tried to contact him. That's when we realized he had never made it to heaven. Until one day, my mom had a vision of him. He told her he was working his way to heaven. His soul was seeking redemption, and he was on a journey to make up for what he'd done. We don't know if he ever made it over, or if he's still working his way to heaven.

He finally realized what he had done and felt remorse during his life review, but being sorry wasn't enough. He had to make amends in heaven.

During the life review, people see the results of their actions from every angle, including the effect it had on their own happiness. The life review is a complete 360-degree representation of everything that went on while you were alive, and it takes into account how you felt, your intentions, the impact that you had on others, and your remorse and regret.

Souls who are truly remorseful will be assigned to do God's work in heaven. Those things are secret, and I'm not allowed to have access to the specifics, but I do pick up clues in my readings that tell me that there are definitely second chances.

When Pain Makes You Bitter and Isolated

A woman once reached out to me on Facebook who was so heartbroken over the death of her son that she was unable to smile and be compassionate to other people. She realized how she was behaving, but felt powerless to stop it. She wrote to me and said she was worried that when she died, she wouldn't get to heaven and see her son again because of how she had treated people after her son passed. I think she was relieved when I explained that God would understand that her grief was the reason for her behavior, he would see that she was sorry for her actions, and would never stop her from being able to reunite with her beloved child.

This woman's dilemma reminds me of people who can't have children and want them so badly that it's impossible for them to be happy for their pregnant friends. They might avoid the baby showers and children's birthday parties, and they may go so far as to cut friends with children out of their lives entirely. These people usually feel guilty for resenting the happy parents who have what they themselves want so badly, but their sense of loss and disappointment is too great to bear. It isn't fair to judge these individuals for being jealous of people with children, because their actions are a result of their own deep pain. That being said, they usually come around eventually and realize that being a friend, godparent, aunt, or uncle to the children in their life can fill the void and bring them joy.

They might take the next step and decide to adopt a child, take in a foster child, or volunteer to help children in some way.

It's comforting to know that even if you stray from your path in life, heaven has a way of returning you to your purest state. When you are born, you arrive on this earth as a pure and perfect being. As you grow, things happen to you, and you absorb the energy that surrounds you. Even if you struggle and act out, that doesn't make you evil. Having seen all the souls who have made it to the other side, I believe that 99.9 percent of humans are good. Sure, some people are bitter, grumpy, and flawed, but only a very tiny percentage are evil.

When Is Someone Truly Evil?

We've spent some time talking about people who act badly for a reason, or who make mistakes but find ways to redeem themselves—either while they are alive or when they complete their life review. But what about those people who don't examine their actions and never have a twinge of concern about the future of their soul? These individuals often feel that anything that helps them get ahead is justified, and if anyone dares to point out the error of their ways they get defensive and angry and refuse to take the criticism seriously. Even during their life review, when they see the results of their actions laid out in front of them, they still can't admit they were wrong.

These souls do have something to worry about. You don't get blocked from heaven because of what you've done, but if you have your review and don't care about the pain and harm you've caused, that's another story. During this part of the chapter, I'm going to share what I know about earthbound spirits, and give you tips on how to keep them from doing damage to you and the people you care about.

Seeking the Light

It's true that earthbound spirits are easier to reach because they are still here—they haven't passed all the way over. Because they exist at a lower vibration, they're easier for a medium to connect with.

Mediums are called mediums for a reason. They have the ability to raise their vibration to connect the high-vibration souls with the lower vibration of human beings on earth. I've often said that mediums are kind of like translators, but they also serve as a stepping-stone between heaven and earth.

People often ask why I don't try to contact earthbound ghosts and spirits and help them pass over. The answer is that I decided to be a medium to help and heal people, and in order to fulfill that mission I have to protect my own energy. For that reason, I make it a point to focus on the light, both in this world and the afterlife, and avoid the darker spirits.

When I was very young, I didn't know how to control my gift, and was often frightened by evil spirits. My grandmother tried to help by explaining that there were high-vibration spirits and low-vibration spirits. She helped me to understand that high-vibration souls are all about love and want the best for people on earth, and the low-vibration spirits just want to bring you down. She even taught me how to filter out the low-vibration spirits by not engaging with them or giving them power. "If you come from light, Matt, you'll always attract light to you," she'd say to me.

That doesn't mean there are not plenty of opportunities for me to dive into the dark side. My phone rings off the hook with invitations from television producers to explore haunted houses and conjure up ghosts and spirits in places where there is negative energy, but I always tell them, "I don't go there!"

Dealing with evil spirits is very much like dealing with evil people on earth. Ninety-nine-point-nine percent of people, living or dead, are basically good, and as far as I'm concerned, it makes sense to avoid the small percentage who are truly evil.

Recognizing Evil

There are living people who thrive on negative energy. They seek it out, absorb it, and share it with their unwilling victims. Because of that, their vibration is very low.

Sometimes you can sense the energy of really evil people. They might even try to influence you to gossip and be unkind to other people. That dark energy is contagious, but you always have the choice to choose light and keep your own energy pure and your vibration high.

Remember that evil spirits are nothing more than the ghosts of evil people who lived in this world. Evil people and evil spirits have a lot in common! Have you ever known someone who seemed like they were out to get you? They spread lies about you, say things to hurt you, and do everything possible to make your life miserable. You can't figure out what motivates them, and assume that they are just mean evil people. But anger comes from pain. Chances are they are so miserable in their own life that they want to bring you down. They might want something you have, and think by keeping you down, they'll get it.

People are attracted to other people's drama because it makes them feel better about themselves. Evil spirits want the same thing. They don't necessarily want to push you down the basement stairs like in a horror movie. What they do want is to steer you away from your own life's path and prevent you from being happy, so they can feel better about themselves.

If there's one thing evil people and negative spirits have in common, it's FEAR! Fear is a low-vibration emotion that blocks you from the higher emotions like compassion and love. It also prevents you from achieving your life purpose.

***

Bad Intentions Can Damage You Without Touching You

There was a woman who was being stalked by an old co-worker. She had been friendly with her at first, until the woman became obsessed with her and the relationship became dark and frightening. It was interfering with her marriage, and she stopped socializing and going out with friends. Instead of enjoying her life, she spent every day in fear, constantly looking over her shoulder. Her co-worker had never touched her or even gotten close to her—but she was controlling her life through fear. The stalker didn't want to physically hurt her; her mission was all about control—and she was winning the battle. Her victim locked herself inside and put big drapes over her windows. Her house was always dark and quiet. She changed her locks and her phone number, and didn't give it out to anyone. She wouldn't share anything on social media, and eventually closed all of her accounts. She lived every day in total paranoia because of her stalker.

One day that woman came to me for a reading, and her mother, who had been watching the situation unfold from the other side, came through immediately. It was during that reading that her mom unveiled the true reason why that woman was stalking her. She could see that her old co-worker was jealous and obsessed with my client. Although the stalker derived a lot of satisfaction from being able to control her victim's life, her mother assured her that the woman would not hurt her. Her mom's advice was to take down the curtains and open the windows. Sure, this person is trying to provoke you, but at the end of the day, she has no power over you. The mother knew for sure that in this case, the stalker would not harm her daughter or her family, and knowing that took away the fear and the power that this woman had to hurt my client.

Just like that stalker, evil spirits want to be known and acknowledged. But you have control of your actions—and reactions. It's like arguing with a negative, angry person. You take the bait and engage with them and what happens? You find yourself rattled, frustrated, and out of breath at the end of your argument, and they're sitting there, satisfied that they've gotten a rise out of you. If you don't engage, you can remove their power to hurt you and become immune to their poison.

Positive and Negative Vibrations

Sometimes people worry that a space is haunted, but it's just energy. Negative energy can feel just like a dark soul or an evil spirit. It can make it appear that a house is haunted, when it's really just old, stale energy that someone left behind. The new homeowners might think they have a ghost or dark spirit, but the problem is easily corrected. If left alone, negative energy can linger for years after the people who created it are gone, but just like turning on a light makes darkness disappear, negative energy can be displaced by positive energy. You can replace it with fresh air, pets, music, and anything that you can think of that represents love and positivity!

If you happen to enter a home, an apartment, or even a hotel room and feel dark, oppressive energy, just open a window, or put up some photos of your family. The more you replace that energy and clear it out, the better the space will feel.

How Hollywood Gets It All Wrong

How many movies have you seen where a happy family moves into their dream house, only to have it become a horrifying nightmare? That situation sells lots of movie tickets, but it's not realistic. Evil spirits don't want to be around happy people. They want to be by themselves. If they happen to be in a house and a new family moves in, they might not leave right away, but in time the new family's energy will displace the evil energy, and the evil spirits will leave.

Caught Between Heaven and Earth

Instead of transitioning over, earthbound spirits stay on earth as invisible dark presences. The chances of coming across these entities in day-to-day life are slim to none, because they like to be alone. They will seek out dark, empty places like abandoned buildings. The last place they want to be is anywhere that happy people are.

Most people think that places are haunted because of what went on there. For example, people think an insane asylum might be permanently tainted because of the pain and madness that existed there for so long. Although it may have a dark history, the real reason is that this empty, desolate space is a perfect place for evil souls to hide. Because these souls are so dark, they have no desire to watch over people or be in the light. Instead, they are happy to take over an empty space where their energy can remain in the shadows.

What Do Evil Spirits Want from Us?

Evil spirits are like the bullies of the afterlife who have nothing better to do than to cause mischief in this world. They didn't take responsibility for the wrong that they did when they were alive, and when they see someone living their best life, they get jealous and want to cause trouble. They feel powerless to move forward and transition to heaven, and they take out that frustration on you. Because they succumbed to negativity and pain in their life, they want to bring you down too.

But they won't pick you out to haunt you unless you go looking for them. I can count on one hand how many people are actually haunted by an evil spirit and those people did something, even if it wasn't intentional, that made them vulnerable to evil. They may have used a Ouija board, or entered a haunted house and conjured up ghosts and dark souls!

Opening the Door to Evil Spirits

People worry that going to a mediumship event can invite evil in, but that's not the case. When you receive a message from a loved one, the medium is creating a direct connection between you, themselves and the soul in heaven. In this case, you know who you're talking to, and they are coming from a place of love. But when you are playing around with a Ouija board, or holding a seance and looking for ghosts, it's like sending out a lighthouse beam that has the potential to attract all kinds of restless beings and dark spirits.

Your guides and loved ones in spirit want to keep you on your path. They want all the good things for you. But the dark souls don't want good things for you. They don't even know you, but they want to transmit their negative energy to you in order to mess with you. They're not happy, and unlike the vast majority of souls in heaven, these earthbound spirits want to splash their unhappiness and negativity all over you!

Every one of us has a destiny that we create with our spirit team before we are born, but we also have free will, and can choose the wrong path. Dark spirits hope that if they are evil, negative, or nasty to you, it will cause you to respond negatively and stray from your own path. Negativity is contagious, but you always have the choice to protect your energy from them.

Is Hell Real?

Does hell exist? I can't say for sure, but based on my experience as a psychic medium, I don't think so. I'm basing my opinion on the fact that I've connected with tens of thousands of souls in heaven and have never heard from a single soul in hell.

SPIRITUAL PRACTICE

WHAT SPIRIT WANTS YOU TO KNOW

There's a life lesson to be learned in all of this. Souls tell me all the time that if they had to do it all over again they wouldn't let any evil into their life. Think of all the time you spent worrying, feeling resentful, or arguing with negative people. Imagine if you didn't let fear into your life. Fear alone won't keep you out of heaven, but it will stop you from creating the life you want in this world.

Exercise: Sending Negativity Packing

This simple technique will help you banish negative energy. Close your eyes and imagine the face of a person who is wishing you harm. Now picture a glowing cord of energy stretching between you and that person. Imagine yourself taking a pair of scissors and snipping the cord. It seems too simple, but if you set your intention it actually works!

You are like a sponge and you absorb all kinds of energy. But just like you can send and receive feelings and thoughts—negative or positive—you can also clear them with your mind. You can also use sage to smoke out negative energy in your space. You have to ask that energy to leave. Let it know that it doesn't have power over you or your home. Open your doors and windows and ask it to leave. Pray to your angels and guides for help. Ask them to surround you as you usher the negativity out of your home. You'll feel a whoosh as they leave, and the air around you will suddenly seem lighter!

Chapter 10

THE PEOPLE YOU MEET IN HEAVEN

The thing I love most about being a spiritual medium is the way my gift allows me to help people heal from loss. An additional benefit I didn't anticipate is this: by proving the existence of life after death and giving people a glimpse of what it's like to transition and go through the life review, I'm able to ease the fear that most of us carry—the fear of dying.

The idea of dying is uncomfortable for most people. Naturally you want to be with your loved ones in a physical sense and continue to live life as you know it. Dying, and leaving all that behind, is scary, but it helps to know that you won't be alone when you make the transition. One of the most important jobs souls in heaven take on is supporting their loved ones in their final hours, and accompanying them on their journey to the other side.

NO ONE DIES ALONE

If you've ever been around someone who is approaching the end of their life, you might notice some unusual behavior. For instance, they might surprise you by nodding, gesturing, or engaging in one-sided conversations with people you can't see. They might reach out their arms or fix their gaze toward an empty place in the room as if someone is there, or casually mention a visit from someone who passed over years earlier.

Actually this behavior isn't strange at all. It's a common practice among the spirit people to show up and help the dying make the transition to the afterlife. It all makes perfect sense when you realize that the "line" that separates the spirit world from the physical world is not a brick wall, but more of a veil. That veil is even more permeable during the times when you are closest to heaven—right after you are born, and as you prepare to make the transition from life to death.

It's common for a dying person to see their mother, father, or some other family member who passed away years before. They might even get a visit from a deceased pet. Often the people around them will think that they are delirious, having side effects from their medication, or not in their right mind, but in fact, they are comforted by the presence of their loved ones who have traveled from the other side to support them through their upcoming transition.

It Wasn't a Hallucination, It Was Virginia!

When my grandfather was dying, I would ask him if anyone had visited him.

He would say, "Matt, you know I didn't have any visitors today."

But one day the nurse came up and said, "Do you know Virginia?" Virginia was his girlfriend who had passed years before. He had introduced her to the nurses (unaware that only he was able to see her) but hadn't said anything to me!

I asked him about it, and he said, "No, no, Virginia wasn't here! I was hallucinating!"

I kept asking him about it, and he would always try to explain it away:

"I was dreaming."

"It was the meds."

"I was just thinking about her, she wasn't here."

My grandfather was totally lucid, and was afraid that if he told people about seeing Virginia, they would think he had dementia.

Even though he wouldn't share any details of his conversations with me, his roommate told me that he could hear him talking to not only Virginia, but his parents and other people who had passed over long before.

Older people are often hesitant to share their visitations or even admit what's happening to themselves. But they do experience them, and if you're open and observant, you'll sense when spirits are around them—either by the dying person's behavior or from signs and sensations from the spirits themselves.

If you are visiting an older friend or relative and you sense this is happening, you might want to ease their mind by letting them know that this is completely normal, and nothing to worry about.

THE SOUL'S JOURNEY TO THE AFTERLIFE

Most people think that the transition of the soul happens when we are officially pronounced dead, but it actually begins before that. People who are dying will often slip into a deep sleep, or a coma-like state. This is the time when loved ones on the other side start to appear to get them ready for their journey. At this point their body is still functioning. Their heart is beating. But their soul is between two worlds.

If you are around someone who is in this state, their eyes may be closed and they won't talk or respond to your voice, but they are aware of what's around them and can still hear your voice. Their soul is starting to transition, and they are no longer fully in their body. They can look down and see their form in the bed, their loved ones, and the room they're in. They have a bird's-eye view of everything that's going on.

This is a time when souls can make certain requests to heaven before transitioning over and their spirit team will be there to help deliver what they ask for.

A Dying Wish

Alexa's stepdad battled a variety of illnesses and in his later years was diagnosed with just about everything you can think of. In the months before he passed, there were several close calls. He was rushed to the hospital on six different occasions in critical condition, but miraculously pulled through and was able to return home after each crisis. Every time, the doctors and nurses would call the family and let us know that it was time to say goodbye, and every time, Alexa and his girls were too afraid to face losing him and wouldn't go. Just for some background, Alexa has always had a hard time stepping foot in a hospital when someone she loves is ill. Even when my mom had cancer surgery, Alexa's fear overcame her and she nearly passed out on the floor.

What ended up happening was that the most recent time he was in the hospital the doctors made the call. This time, Alexa stayed pretty calm. There had been so many false alarms that she expected him to make it out again. But as the morning went on, she couldn't stop thinking about him.

Suddenly we were in the drive-through line at Starbucks and she looked at me and said, "We have to go to the hospital!" Her anxiety had suddenly vanished, and all she knew was that something was compelling her to get to his bedside. She didn't understand why her fears had vanished or why she felt it was so critical that she get there. I trusted her intuition and backed the car around. Royce was in the back seat, and her only concern was that he not be frightened.

We arrived at the hospital, and I took Royce out of his car seat. Alexa was running ahead, which was very out of character for her!

We went into Alexa's stepdad's room and he was completely unresponsive. The monitors showed that he was breathing, but his eyes were shut and he didn't respond when we spoke to him.

I assured Alexa that he could still see and hear everything that was going on even though it looked like he was completely out of it. While this was going on, Royce kept staring at him intensely, as if he was looking straight into his soul. I sensed that Royce was able to see his true self, not the sick person in the bed.

Without any of the anxiety she usually displayed in hospitals, Alexa hugged her stepdad and shared some final messages that she had been holding in for some time. By now, some other family members had arrived, and we decided to step out to give them some private time with him. I looked at my watch and said to Alexa, "Let's give them ten minutes and we will go back in."

We were in the lobby. Ten minutes had passed, and I asked Alexa if she was ready to go back in.

She looked at me calmly. "I'm fine, I did everything I needed to do. I don't think there's anything left. I'm going to wait in the car."

I went inside to say my goodbyes, but a family member came up to me and said, "I don't think that he's breathing." I went to the bed and listened to his chest, and he had passed away.

The timing of this was no accident. He had waited for everyone to be there before he drew his final breath. Alexa had that sense of peace that she had said everything she needed to say.

Later that night, Alexa asked me why I thought she was overcome by that strong feeling. I told her what I had felt as the situation was happening. I was sure he had reached out to her because he knew she was too scared to go and see him. He had to see her one more time to say goodbye, and he knew she had to find the courage to enter the hospital. That was his last request, and heaven made it happen.

Death Without Fear: What Souls Experience in Their Final Hours

Most of us have known at least one person who was so afraid of death that they wouldn't even talk about it. You could never joke around about dying, and they wouldn't make plans or preparations for a funeral or memorial because they just could not go there! Yet as they approached death, their fear disappeared.

What I've learned from souls on the other side is that even though a person might be afraid at the thought of dying, at the end they enter a dreamlike state. Suddenly their fear dissolves and they become very detached from life. Their deceased loved ones are there to comfort them and escort them through the veil, and they peacefully slip away. The weirdest thing about dying is that you don't actually know what's happening when you're going through it. When I talk to a soul who has passed away many times, they don't even realize they've passed.

It's like when you fall asleep. The other night, I was watching a movie and I fell asleep. I woke up and I couldn't remember falling asleep, or what happened in the movie I'd been watching. All I knew was that I woke up totally refreshed.

People say to me, "I don't want to die because I can't imagine not being a physical being. I will miss my body!" They imagine that dying is something you have to fight off. But think of when you're dreaming. You don't miss being awake. You don't worry about where you are, or even know that you're dreaming. You just accept the experience for what it is.

Transitioning isn't like opening a door, or getting off an airplane and being in another country. It's more like when you wake up from a dream and for that moment between being asleep and being fully awake you ask yourself, "Did that really happen?"

I promise, when you arrive in heaven you won't be freaked out and wondering, *Where the heck am I?!* Souls have no fear and won't even be fully aware that they are no longer alive.

In fact, when you arrive in heaven you will feel pure peace and joy as you're reunited with dozens of loved ones and pets who passed away before you.

A Glimpse into the Future Can Put
Your Fears to Rest

When a soul is transitioning, they will typically have some questions and concerns—not for themselves, but for the loved ones they left behind. The following are typical of these.

› Is my daughter going to be okay? She's going through a divorce and she needs me!

› Does this mean I'll never meet my grandchildren or attend my son's wedding?

› Who will take care of my spouse? There are still some important things I need to tell them.

Fortunately souls are not left wondering and worrying. They have access to all the knowledge in the universe, and can clearly see the answers to their questions. In fact, they will have more insight than they could possibly have had in life. For example, a mother worried about her daughter's dissolving marriage will get a glimpse of how things will ultimately work out, even before the actual divorce is finalized.

That's why in a reading, souls can often forecast the future and give their loved one peace of mind, or advice to help them navigate the situation.

At a recent event, I did a reading for a husband who had lost his wife. She had just turned forty when she was diagnosed with inoperable brain cancer. The woman had been terrified of dying because she didn't want to leave her children without a mom. She fought as hard as she could, but the cancer was too powerful, and she passed when her children were barely four and five years old.

During the reading, she came through and shared what had happened in her final hours. Her husband got so much comfort from her message, and I could see how everyone in the audience was moved by her words. She told me that when her loved ones came to get her and accompany her to heaven, she expressed her fear and sadness about leaving her children behind. Like any good mother, she hated the thought of leaving them. To ease her mind, they showed her the future. She saw them as they were when she died, and was able to "fast-forward" as they grew and matured. She got a beautiful preview of her daughter getting married years later, and her son graduating college, and was gratified to see the happy expressions on their faces. At that point she knew then that she didn't have to worry. She could see visions of the future and knew they would be okay.

MEETING YOUR WELCOMING COMMITTEE

I've asked Spirit what it feels like when you get to heaven, and based on what they've shown me, I have a clear picture of what the experience is like. I think this will help you understand what happens better.

Have you ever gone to a high school reunion, and at first, you're wondering who those people are? They look familiar, but it's not until you talk to them the memories start flooding back. Suddenly, after a few minutes, you are right back to where you were twenty-five years ago. Heaven feels like that. You see these souls and they are so familiar, and you realize that they were an important part of your life—and still are a part of your soul family!

Everyone Has a Soul Family in Heaven

Sometimes people worry that if a baby or child passes away, they won't have anyone to meet them in heaven. If that child never lost anyone in their short life, would they be all alone? It's not like a person who grew up with their parents and grandparents and lost them—then got reunited in heaven. But rest assured, even babies who die without knowing a single soul have people waiting for them in heaven. Those souls might not have known them in the physical world, but remember—those babies and young children were with their family in heaven before they were born, and will be reunited with them.

Being Reunited with Your Pets

Your dearly departed loved ones aren't the only ones you meet in heaven. You also are introduced to your spirit guides and angels, and the pets you shared your life with. They all gather to welcome you to heaven and support you during your transition.

It's even more wonderful to be reunited with your pets than you might expect, because suddenly you're connecting at a soul-to-soul level. In heaven, animals have the same access to universal knowledge as any other soul.

One of the things that freaks me out, even after years of being a medium, is that pets can actually speak to us in the afterlife. It makes sense because no matter what their nationality or species, all spirits can communicate with one another. Someone who spoke Greek when they were alive can talk to someone who spoke Italian and communicate perfectly. It's the same with our pets—they can speak full sentences and communicate just like people. That's why I can share messages from your pets during a reading. People are sometimes surprised by what their pet remembers (they suddenly understand the reasons for the vet visits, etc.) and who they are with in heaven.

When dogs and cats are alive in this world they have no concept of money or time, but when they die, they gain a new understanding and perspective. Here's an example from a recent reading that brings this point home:

> A woman had a dog who was like a child to her. The dog had a heart issue, and when she brought him to the vet, he told her she could pay for an expensive operation that might give the dog another year or two. She didn't have much money, but she loved the dog so much that she tapped into her 401(k) to pay for the $12,000 operation. Even

though the surgery went well, her dog passed away shortly after. She didn't regret the surgery or second-guess herself. Even though his life was cut short, she had taken the chance willingly for more time with her beloved dog.

While he was alive, her dog didn't understand the magnitude of what she had done for him. Our animals can't possibly understand what we go through when they get sick. They don't understand the sacrifices we make out of our love for them—at least not while they are alive. But after they die, they tap into the universal knowledge and get the whole story. During my readings, I've seen many examples of pets coming back and thanking their owners for the love and care they showered on them and the sacrifices they made to give them the best care possible.

When my own cat got sick, she was only three years old. For six months, I brought her to the vet for chemo and cared for her at home. The poor cat didn't know why I was taking her to the vet so often. She hated getting her skin pinched, and being administered pills and injections. It wasn't until she finally passed over that she understood what I'd been doing and that I'd been taking care of her.

————

It's the Soul That Counts

Even though your dog or cat feels like a member of your family, you might wonder about their biological family—the mother who gave birth to them and the littermates they shared their first weeks of life with. What happens to those animal families in the afterlife? The answer is that while your pets will see their animal family members in heaven, they don't have the same strong soul connection that they have with you. When you adopt a pet into your life and they become part of your family, something happens that I like to call "soul reassignment."

Humans and animals have this in common. While everyone has a biological family, that isn't necessarily your strongest bond. In heaven, people who are adopted have biological parents, but the people who they saw as their family—the adoptive parents who cared for them and raised them—are the people they will be with in heaven. Your pets are part of your soul family, and that's why they wait with the rest of your soul family for you to join them in heaven.

That's why sometimes family members will be with a cat or dog in heaven that they never knew in life—you adopted them into your soul family, and they will be part of the family group that is together in the afterlife.

Love Keeps Us Together!

We've talked about how hard it is to leave your loved ones behind, or to lose a parent, child, or pet when they cross over. But love is the strongest bond there is, and it can't be broken by death. Your loved ones watch over you in life, and wait to help you transition over when it's your time to go. Heaven is a place that reunites you with the people you love; it doesn't separate you.

People are nervous that when they die they will go back to the blood-line, not the heart. But life in heaven is about the true, strong connection of love. If your stepfather or adoptive mother was a loving part of your life and was the person you saw as a parent, that same bond will endure in heaven. It's the same with your pets. Your dog won't be with his litter-mates, but with the pets and people he lived with, protected, and loved.

SPIRITUAL PRACTICE:

HOMEWORK FROM HEAVEN:
GETTING CLOSER TO YOUR SOUL FAMILY

You might not know exactly which souls will walk you across the tunnel of light when your time comes, but you can get a peek at the "guest list" by asking those guides, angels, and loved ones to reveal themselves to you. Here's how!

Gather some photographs of family members who are no longer among the living. Maybe your mom has an old album with photos from holidays and special gatherings, or a wedding portrait with a large group of friends and family. Take some time to gaze at the faces while opening yourself up to guidance. Think about each person, say their name out loud, and replay some of the interactions you've had with them. As you revisit those memories, pay attention to the ones that stand out the most. Invite the souls who are now deceased to visit you in your dreams, or send you a sign. Keep a journal to note how the souls make their presence known. The ones that stand out in your mind as you practice this exercise, or that visit you in your dreams, will also be the ones who help ease you out of life and escort you to heaven.

WHAT SPIRIT WANTS YOU TO KNOW

The thought of dying is scary, but the more you know about the afterlife, the more control you can have of that fear. In fact, sometimes the things you are most worried about turn out to be an unexpected blessing. For instance, there was a man who came through to me in a reading. He had been sick and in pain every single day of his life. He told me he had been so afraid to die, and thought, *If I'm in this much pain now, imagine what it will be like to pass away.* The struggle with his health went beyond the physical. He suffered from emotional pain because his poor health kept him from fully participating and enjoying family celebrations and holidays. He never felt good and always had to leave events early. When he finally passed over, he was a completely different person. He had been sick for so much of his life that he never knew what it was like to experience life without illness. Now, in his spirit form, he was able to be around events with family on earth and found himself experiencing so much joy watching over his loved ones without the burden of his poor health.

In this chapter, we started off talking about how your loved ones in heaven help ease the pain and fear of death, and wrapped it up by talking about how your pets will be waiting for you when you pass. Again and again, as I connect with souls in heaven, I witness the powerful, unbreakable connection of love. As my friends on the other side constantly remind me, the more you can believe in that and embrace it, the less scary death becomes.

Chapter 11

THE LIFE REVIEW

Over the last ten chapters, we've considered the life review from just about every angle. By now, you understand what is revealed at this time, and how you can make amends in the afterlife for harm you may have done when you were on earth. You can clearly see how looking back on your life from heaven puts everything in a new perspective. However, it still might be difficult to truly imagine what will actually take place when you sit down with your spirit team and revisit every relationship, action, and path taken (and not taken).

In this chapter I'm going to walk you, step by step, through what really happens during an actual life review. How do I know? I've never "officially" visited heaven, but as a medium, I've gained glimpses of this enlightening event through the eyes of countless souls who have gone through it.

WHO'S RUNNING THE SHOW?

If you're wondering who will be conducting your life review after you pass over, look in the mirror. No being, mortal or divine, living or dead, is more qualified than your own soul to run the meeting! Deep within you there is a "ledger" that contains every moment of your life. Now it's time to sit back and see things through a crystal-clear lens as revealed by your true self. If that sounds overwhelming, don't worry. You won't be alone. Sitting beside you will be your loved ones in heaven, angels, and guides, gathered to watch a documentary of your life. Together you'll not only see what happened, but you'll go deeper into the impact you had on others, and explore what might have been and other roads you would have taken.

What Is the Setting of Your Life Review?

You might imagine yourself during your life review, sitting in a conference room with one of those big speakerphones in the middle of the table and a PowerPoint displayed on the screen. If you have spent time in a corporate job, I get why that image would come to mind, but it's not like that! Instead, visualize yourself putting on virtual reality glasses and walking through the moments of your life as if it were the ultimate spiritual video game, where you can see what happens and what might have been. However, unlike with a video game, you won't be able to change things as you go. Those events are in the past, and there's no going back—but you will be able to see everything that you experienced, from all angles, all at once. And there will be time to make amends in the afterlife!

How Long Does the Life Review Take?

I guess the first thing that comes to mind when I think about the length of a life review is, *Do you have somewhere else to be?*

Seriously, it might seem like it would take a long time to revisit your entire existence, but it goes by in a few seconds. Some people experience more and live a fuller life and their review takes longer. And remember, when you're in heaven, time takes on a different meaning.

Bookends: Marking the Beginning and End of Life

In the first chapter, we talked about how your team in heaven prepares you to be born. Everyone comes together to get you ready for the send-off.

When you first arrive on earth, it must feel to your soul family in heaven like they're sending a child off to college. They're looking forward to watching your progress and seeing your soul learn and flourish as you experience life lessons and earn your "degree."

Just like attending a college graduation, when your spirit team welcomes you home, like we talked about in the last chapter, it's not the end. You simply take that wisdom that you learned in life, and apply it to the next chapter of your soul's journey.

To get the most out of any kind of educational experience, you have to assess and examine what you learned. That's where the life review comes in!

Check Your Baggage at the Gates

As a medium, I don't only get messages from the other side. Souls often show me images of what life is like in heaven, and they do so for a good reason.

They want everyone to know that life on earth isn't all there is! Providing proof of the afterlife is a wonderful gift souls give to the living to help alleviate the fear of dying, and as a medium, I'm happy to help them share the word.

I was searching for a way to illustrate how heaven, life, and the afterlife flow together, and I was a little bit stuck. I asked my guides to help, and sure enough, the answer was provided to me as I was dragging my suitcase through the airport, and it struck me that a soul's journey to heaven had some things in common with the experience I was having. See if this helps you visualize your spiritual journey. . . .

Your first arrival into heaven is like showing up at the airport before a trip. You check your heavy luggage, and then you go through TSA and they make sure you don't have anything that can't go on the plane. You don't argue with the TSA person, because you know that it will be easier for you, and better for the other people on the plane if you just carry the essentials, and leave behind or "check" what you don't need.

When you buy your ticket and prepare to board the plane, you and the other souls sharing the space with you have agreed to the code of conduct, which includes leaving behind not just physical items but behaviors.

You're not forced to do these things—but if you don't agree you can't get on the plane and move on to your next destination. At the end of life, you have only your soul to "carry on."

The Tunnel of White Light Opens

When your soul leaves your body, it's a peaceful thing. I remember having wisdom teeth surgery, and I was in so much pain, but as soon as I drifted off to sleep I couldn't feel the pain. In fact, it might have been the meds, but in my anesthetized state, I thought I was eating a big meal! There was no pain until I woke up and my mouth was still sore and packed with cotton. But for those few moments, I was able to escape the anxiety, pain, and discomfort I had been feeling.

Souls experience this when they go through the tunnel of white light. The soul lifts off from the physical body, just like in a dream. People don't even realize they are passing, but they feel comforted and reassured because they can see the people who have passed on before them.

When you transition, there is a tunnel that opens up in heaven for your soul to pass through. You leave behind the earthly things that you were attached to—and the things that were weighing you down. You release illness, pain, suppressed emotions, childhood trauma, grudges, resentment, and anything that has caused you pain. You carry with you one thing only—your true essence!

As you travel through the tunnel, every memory comes flooding back—including the time you spent in heaven before you were born. Suddenly your whole life starts to make sense. You realize the place you are entering is familiar to you and so are the people that are there. You are not afraid, because it suddenly becomes crystal clear that you are not leaving earth, but going home.

REUNITING WITH TWO DIVINE BEINGS

When you get to heaven, you meet up with your main spirit guide and your guardian angel. You recognize them at a soul level. You may not recall exactly how you know them, but trust me: they will be familiar to you. It's like when you meet distant family members, and you feel a kinship to them, even though you don't recall spending time with them in life.

You're not surprised when they explain to you that they have been with you all along—silently guiding you and helping you. You know in your heart that it's true, and you realize that's the reason their presence seems so familiar.

Glimpses from Heaven

The messages and images I've received from souls in the afterlife blend together in my mind like a beautiful collage, revealing what the afterlife is like and what takes place during the life review. I wish I could share it all with you, but I'll do the next best thing: pull back the curtain and share an example of the life review that souls have shared.

Opportunities lost—the road not taken.

During his life review, an alcoholic sees every crossroad, and every opportunity he has to change course. He sees himself taking his first drink, when he learned how drinking helped him feel more comfortable socially. Then he watches as he begins to abuse alcohol to numb a sense of isolation and sadness. Pictures flash before him like a slideshow. He's sitting in an AA meeting but pushes away his sponsor's offer to help and leaves before the meeting adjourns. "This isn't me," he tells himself. "I'm not a train wreck like these losers." Now he gets a glimpse of how his life would have been different if he had stayed in that meeting. He sees how his sponsor becomes his best friend. They help each other stay sober. He is sober at his daughter's wedding and gives her away. Then he flashes back to reality. He is estranged from most of his family, and fights with the ones still around. He messes up at work. But there's a light at the end of the tunnel. Even though his life is over, it's not too late to make amends. From the afterlife, he can help his children to heal. He sees his daughter putting up walls to avoid being hurt again, and his son masking his own pain through alcohol and pills. He knows his purpose in the afterlife. His job will be to steer his children onto the right path and help other addicts to get the help they need.

Your life matters.

A teacher whose life was cut short had loved children from the time she was a teenager. She spent as much time with them as possible, working as a babysitter, then a camp counselor. After college, she got her credentials and went on to be a teacher. She died young in an accident, and her final regret on her deathbed was that she never had her own children. However, in her life review she sees how many lives she touched as a teacher. She realizes that so many of the children in her class carry the memory of her care and nurturing. She realizes that she made a difference in their lives. Her life may have been far too short, but she is comforted knowing that the ripple effect of her work on earth continues to live on. In the afterlife, she will be able to continue the work she loves by watching over her students. She hopes to guide and inspire some of them to follow in her footsteps, and have a positive influence on children as babysitters, teachers, and parents.

An eye-opening experience.

A woman fell into a deep depression after losing her son. She refused to celebrate holidays, neglected her other children, and spent the remainder of her life a bitter, cold, miserable person. She remained totally shut down, afraid of getting hurt again, until she got to heaven and saw her son there. His soul was light and happy as he looked down on his friends and family. If she had known her son was not only fine in heaven, but watching over her, she would have lived her life differently, secure in knowing that she would see him again. This is why souls come back and encourage us to live our lives differently. That's why mediums can help and heal the living by demonstrating that life as we know it is just the beginning, and that our loved ones live on in the afterlife.

Guides and angels were there all the time.

There was a woman who came through in a reading and told me about an event that had happened to her years before she died. The woman had gone out clubbing and had too much to drink. Unaware of how intoxicated she actually was, she went to the parking lot and found out her car had been towed. She was angry and upset when it happened, but told me that during her life review, she learned it was actually her guides looking out for her. She called a friend and got driven home safely. It wasn't till she passed and looked back over her life that she saw what could have happened. It turns out that by having her car towed, her guides had intervened and saved not only her life, but the lives of other people with whom she would have collided if she had gotten in her car.

Things You Might Learn in Your Life Review

Every life review is different, but there are some common themes that come up again and again. As you review these, open your mind and ask yourself what insights you could pick up TODAY, while you're still alive, to help you live your very best life on earth. Remember, you don't have to wait till you're dead to clearly see and understand:

› The good things you did in your life

› The things you did that hurt other people—
  and yourself

› The people you let down

> The people you helped

> The lessons you learned

> The lies you told yourself

> The opportunities you missed

> How many chances you took

> How fear held you back

> Your best and worst traits

> How your spirit guides helped you

> How your angels protected you

> The people you met that betrayed you

> The people you should have forgiven

> The people who changed the course of your life

> The love you shared and the moments that truly
> mattered

As you consider your life as it is right now, please know that you're here for a reason! Even if you think your life is uneventful and ordinary, you have the chance to take a leap or spark inspiration for someone around you.

So many conditions we deal with in our lives create a filter that clouds our vision and holds us back. That filter might be fear, pain, trauma, hurt, or addiction. When you die, that filter is gone, along with the condition that created it. Suddenly you can see the real picture! But remember, I'm writing this book to tell you that you don't have to wait till you're dead to clean off that filter and see life through a clear, compassionate lens.

SPIRITUAL PRACTICE

HOMEWORK FROM HEAVEN

Refusing to forgive someone for a small slight or waiting for them to make the first move to mend your relationship just means you have to carry that heavy grudge around with you. Put down your burden and reach out. Send a greeting card to three people you have had disagreements with, and tell them you love and miss them. Don't dwell on the past, just open your heart and envision happier times ahead.

Now, if the person has really done something terrible, you don't have to let them back into your life—but it will help YOU in the long run if you let go and move on. So go ahead: write the letter and express your feelings. Then seal it up and don't send it! Toss it in the trash, burn it, or tuck it away. But when you close the envelope, release your anger and tell yourself, "I'm making the choice to forgive, for my own sake!"

WHAT SPIRIT WANTS YOU TO KNOW

When souls come through after death by suicide, they often have regrets. The fact that I connect with so many souls who have died in this way proves that they do in fact go to heaven, but it's a hard road.

Oftentimes, this can be difficult for people to understand. They wonder, why would souls have regrets if they are at peace?

Part of the life review process is that in addition to seeing the events of our life from our own perspective, we also see how our behavior and the choices we made affected other people. With suicide, the regret often comes when the souls see how their death caused so much pain, guilt, and agony for their friends, family, and children.

Although they may be at peace in the spirit world, they can see how their death haunts so many who are still living in trying to navigate their own path through life. Although they may have found peace in heaven, it's hard for them to see their loved ones still struggling after their passing.

Not only that, but during the life review they see how their lives would have turned out if they had kept on going. It's like an actor who keeps auditioning and not getting the part, and finally gives up on their dream and gets an office job. Imagine if they had a way of seeing, after the fact, that if they had gone on one more casting call, they would have gotten the role and their whole life would have changed! That often happens to people who are victims of suicide. They look back on what might have been, and see themselves meeting their soul mate, finding a great doctor who helps them overcome depression, or in some way continuing on and having a good life. We can learn a lot from suicide victims. While we are alive, we are so focused on the now, and the challenges and problems we're facing.

As humans we are stuck in the moment. People come to me with the biggest stressors: *I'm about to lose my job. I can't pay my bills. My son is flunking out of school.* When I connect them with their loved ones in heaven, everything gets calmer, because they can see that the problems that seem so huge and insurmountable are just a temporary challenge. Spirit shows them that there are good things ahead if they hang in there and let their team in heaven help and guide them.

Chapter 12

THE FINAL CHAPTER

Congratulations—you've made it to the final chapter! I believe Spirit has provided me with this information for one reason . . . to help you see that *you don't have to wait till you're dead.*

Souls who have gone before want to help you start living a better life right now—while you're still alive. All you need is an open heart and the insights that souls in heaven have revealed to me that I'm sharing with you in this book.

Right now you might be thinking, *What if I could perform my own life review now, while I'm still here, living, breathing, and able to make changes?*

Well, if that's what you're wondering, rest assured that Spirit is already one step ahead of you! Keep reading for instructions and questions to help you get started on your own life review right now. . . .

Before you dive into these enlightening exercises, take a moment to prepare your mind, body, and spirit for the profound emotional journey you're about to embark on. Start by finding a quiet space where you won't be disturbed: a comfortable chair, a bench in your backyard, or sitting up against the headboard of your bed.

When you've found a place and settled in, close your eyes and focus on your breathing, relaxing more deeply with each breath. As you settle into a calm, focused, state, clear your mind of any distractions or concerns. You're about to engage in your very own life review—a sacred, spiritual, and deeply emotional process that can bring immense insight, clarity, and healing.

When you feel centered and relaxed, begin by asking yourself the first question in each exercise and allow your inner wisdom to guide your answers. If you feel stuck, you can call upon your angels, loved ones, and spirit guides by asking them to stay by your side as you revisit deep and emotional moments from your time on earth.

Exercise 1: How Earthly Life Has Shaped You

Seeing life through a child's eyes gives us a glimpse of pure innocence. Children are untouched by greed, judgment, guilt, or pain. Their hearts are open and their spirits are free and all they know is love. Spirit tells us that although we may learn bad behavior here on earth, the path back to being a pure soul is always within reach and we can start over on a clean slate.

Think about what you were like as a child. Were you shy, joyful, smiling, laughing? Remember how you looked, and the way you saw the world. Everything was big and exciting. The simple things in life, like a stuffed animal or an ice cream cone, would bring you endless amounts of joy. How was life so simple?

Reflection:

› As you started to become older, what factors in life started influencing your behavior and thoughts?

› How did expectations from your family or lack thereof affect the person you grew to be?

› How did peer pressure or the people around you affect you?

› As an adult, how have you changed in order to fit in with society?

› Finally, think about positive steps you can take to get back to your original pure soul self. These could be as simple as dedicating time to activities that genuinely bring you joy, or as complex as reconsidering your life choices and relationships.

Now that you've had time to consider these questions, grab your journal or a piece of paper and write down the key insights, memories, and observations that stand out to you.

_____

_____

_____

_____

_____

_____

_____

Exercise 2: Recognize Your Innate Talents

Recognizing your God-given talents, gifts, and strengths is the first step toward a life lived in alignment with your spiritual purpose. Your talents are not random; they are precious gifts meant to serve you and others and to help make positive changes here in this world.

Reflection:

Take a moment to think about yourself as a child.

› What were you naturally good at?

› When you played as a child, where did your imagination take you?

Close your eyes and take a journey back in time to your childhood playgrounds, classrooms, and homes. What role did you play? Were you a natural healer and helping people, a teacher teaching students, or a singer performing in front of millions of people? Or perhaps you were the mediator among friends, the one who could easily resolve conflicts and maintain harmony.

Take a moment to think. Use the lines below to relive these memories and rediscover your purpose in life.

Exercise 3: Regrets and Redemption

Regret can either be a heavy burden or a powerful motivator for change. By recognizing and addressing your regrets, you can free your soul from unnecessary weight and sadness. Allowing yourself to be burdened by guilt and pain is like choosing to wear heavy winter clothes in the middle of summer. As you take off each layer, the lighter you feel in your body and soul. In this reflection we will remove each piece of clothing and our burden layer by layer . . .

Reflection:

Close your eyes and take a deep breath. Look back on your life and allow the regrets to bubble up to the surface. They might be small regrets, like cheating on a math exam in the fourth grade, or bigger ones, like cheating on a spouse or a significant other. Each of these regrets is heavy and has been weighing on you from the time it happened. Think of how these regrets have haunted you and caused you pain in your life. Think about what you could have done differently and what you would do now if you were in that same situation. Now, imagine ways that you can find redemption. Could you apologize or reach out to a person you wronged? Could you turn your experience into a lesson and share it with others? What changes could you make in your life now that would serve as a way to pay it forward? When you recognize your regrets and use them to help warn or teach others, you are releasing the burden and turning a negative experience into something more positive.

Take a moment to create a plan on how you can change past regrets into useful ways to help and teach others.

Exercise 4: Using 20/20 Hindsight

Spirit tells me that during their life review they can see how their challenges, struggles, and letdowns have actually made them stronger, wiser, and more compassionate. Despite the twists and turns that they took in life, they ended up exactly where they needed to be, even if it took longer than expected. While the experiences may have been difficult, they made us who we are today.

Reflection:

Close your eyes and breathe in and out. Open your mind and think about the challenging times you faced as you focus on these words: *financial, physical, emotional, mental, love.* What words have the most pain attached to them as you think about them? What were the circumstances that caused you the most pain? Was it going through bankruptcy, ending a relationship, having an emotional breakdown, or losing a job?

Now, think about the lesson your spirit guides might have been trying to teach you with each event. Looking back, how did this shape your future decisions and who you are today? If you are still going through this, what do you think your guide is trying to show you? The lesson might be about empathy, love, compassion, inner strength, courage, or forgiveness. Take a minute to write down each challenge and the corresponding lesson it taught you in the lines below. By doing this, you will start to see how far you have come,

how much you have grown, and how you can continue to
learn from adversity.

_____

_____

_____

_____

_____

_____

_____

_____

_____

_____

_____

_____

_____

Exercise 5: Releasing Limiting Beliefs

Spirit tells me that we are the only ones that can create our dream life and find our own happiness. However, our minds often get in the way and try to convince us otherwise. A limiting belief is like an invisible fence that stops you from being your true best self. Thoughts like *That will never happen for me*, or thinking you are not good enough, can create fear, which can block the good things that are meant to enter your life.

Reflection:

Close your eyes and breathe in and out. Take a moment to think of these areas of your life: career, family, love, finance, health. As you reflect on these areas, think about your "wish list": the things you want for yourself that you fear you'll never have. Those "never have" feelings are your limiting beliefs. Ask yourself, are these limiting beliefs really TRUE? How would you live your life differently if these negative thoughts didn't exist within you? Identify and challenge each belief by thinking about the advice your spirit guide and guardian angel would give to you in heaven.

Exercise 6: Your Team in Heaven

Life is challenging and difficult, but fortunately you don't have to experience the challenges and struggles alone. Your angels, loved ones, and spirit guides are with you. When you welcome them into your life, you will recognize all the wonderful ways they are helping you, guiding you, and teaching you. Sometimes it's not until you look back that you realize they have been there all along . . .

Reflection:

Take a moment to focus on and answer the following questions.

› Have there been specific moments in your life where you were in danger and felt that something or someone had saved you? For example, did you fall down the stairs and suffer no injuries? Almost drowned, and someone unexpectedly saved you?

› Have you experienced certain signs during times that you were missing a loved one or at significant times in your life? Signs like dragonflies, butterflies, dreams, or repeating numbers?

› If you could communicate with your team in heaven, what questions would you ask? What guidance do you feel you need right now in your life?

› When was the last time you felt something was divinely meant to be? Something that made you question the chances? For example, did you ever experience a lucky event or synchronicity so powerful and impactful that it could be classified as a miracle?

_____

_____

_____

_____

_____

_____

_____

_____

_____

_____

_____

_____

_____

_____

Exercise 7: Second Chances

Your spirit guide has a knack for redirecting you and getting your attention when you are about to make a bad decision. These events are known as "wake-up calls." A health scare, the loss of a job, or a moment that shakes you up inside might be a divine sign that it is time to rethink and refocus on your life. Some wake-up calls can be powerful enough to make you rethink your entire life. Think of your own wake-up calls you experienced and consider their significance.

Close your eyes and take deep breaths in and out. Have you ever had a moment that shook you to your core? Maybe you saw your life flash before your eyes or became emotional as you pondered the meaning of your life. What did this experience teach you and how did it change you? How has this helped you redirect your pathway in life?

_____

_____

_____

_____

_____

Exercise 8: The Power of Forgiveness

Forgiving can be the hardest thing to do, but it can also be the most spiritually rewarding gift you can imagine. The things that are the hardest to face and forgive will release the most pain. Often we hold on to grudges, resentment, and hurt because we believe we are protecting ourselves and our spirit from pain, when really we are keeping those feelings alive by holding on to them. When you forgive, you no longer allow the residual pain caused by other people to control or influence your life. Forgiveness does not have to be a phone call or letter. It can be as simple as recognizing the pain and releasing it.

Reflection:

Take a moment to answer the following questions. It is important that you answer each question on paper. As you write, imagine the pain flowing from your body and attaching itself to the paper. The painful events will be safe in this book. The act of writing out each question is a natural way to release the pain and let out the hurt you have been holding in.

> › Who is the family member that you find it the hardest to forgive? How did they hurt you or break your trust?

> › Are you mad at yourself? What are you having a hard time forgiving yourself for? Recall these regrets without judgment, just as a witness to your life.

› When hearing the words *anger*, *guilt*, and *pain*, what person or situation comes to mind?

› Imagine trying to walk with a heavy sandbag tied to each one of your shoes. The more you walk, the heavier they feel and become. Imagine what it would feel like to cut the cord and let go.

› Take a moment and imagine cutting the energy cord between you and the person, situation, or life event that is causing you past pain. Take a moment to internalize forgiving that person or yourself. Cut the cord and release the energy.

Exercise 9: Heaven Sent—Teacher, Friend, and Foe

Everyone you meet within your life has a greater meaning. Whether their job is to teach us a lesson, guide us on our life path, or simply to provide love and support, the people we encounter often have a higher purpose and significant places within our lives. Let's revisit some of the key and influential people in your life and figure out why heaven divinely felt you should meet.

Reflection:

› Who are the people in your life who've had a profound impact on you? List family, teachers, friends, and foes.

› For each person listed, what specific qualities or actions made their impact so significant? Was it their empathy, love, kindness, or something more negative?

› Do you feel any of these people were "heaven-sent" at a particular moment in your life? Think about where you were at the time in your life when you met them or how they were significant to you.

› Were there any lessons, skills, or insights you gained from these relationships? This could be how to cook, how to be a better person, or how to have empathy.

› Why do you think heaven introduced you to these people?
Use your intuition and write the first thing that comes to
mind.

_____

_____

_____

_____

_____

_____

_____

_____

_____

_____

Exercise 10: Meeting in Heaven

One of the most amazing aspects of the spirit world is that one day we will be reunited with everyone we have loved and missed so dearly. Friends, family, and even our pets are there waiting for us. The final journey of the life review is meeting your loved ones again, so take a moment now to envision that reunion.

Reflection:

Close your eyes and imagine yourself arriving in heaven. Take a moment to think about what heaven looks and feels like to you. What would the perfect world look like?

Who are the first souls you expect to see as you arrive? Would it be family, friends, pets, or perhaps spiritual guides? Picture their faces and their joyful, loving energy welcoming you. Imagine the initial moments, the hugs, the laughter, and the tears of joy.

Exchanging Stories: What would you share with them? Imagine yourself discussing meaningful life events and lessons learned. What would you talk about?

Universal Knowledge: What universal wisdom, lessons learned, or insights would you want to share with your loved ones? Describe the spiritual growth or earthly achievements you're most proud of.

Questions: What would you ask them? Is there a burning question that you've always wanted to have answered?

Legacy Left Behind: What do you want them to know about the legacy you've left on earth? Would you like them to be aware of the love you spread, the lives you touched, or specific accomplishments?

CONCLUSION

Open your eyes and take some time to journal these reflections. This exercise can offer a profound sense of what's truly important in life, what relationships need nurturing now, and what achievements would make you feel most fulfilled when your earthly journey is complete. Review your notes often as a reminder to live a life that makes for a joyous heavenly reunion.

_____

_____

_____

_____

_____

_____

_____

ACKNOWLEDGMENTS

Wow! As I write these words I cannot believe that I am now a *New York Times* bestselling author and on to my third book with the incredible team at Simon & Schuster and Gallery Books. This would all not be possible without the amazing team I have by my side!

To my wife, Alexa, I love you so much! Thank you for being so supportive of me and for allowing me to share my gift with the world. Knowing I have your love and support keeps me going even through the toughest moments.

To my son, Royce, thank you for sharing your dad with the world and for waiting for me to come home from every tour stop. My joy is seeing you and Mommy.

Heartfelt thanks to my mother, Angela, my father, Roderick, and my sister, Maria. From the reality show to everyday life, I am so happy to have you with me on this journey.

Imal Wagner, my esteemed publicist for over a decade! Look how far we've come! From our first book to now, your belief in me has turned dreams into realities, including a reality TV series and noteworthy media appearances. You've been the architect of my career, and for that I am forever grateful.

Ricardo Couto, my tour manager extraordinaire, your huge support, positive attitude, and dedication have made our national tours not only successful but memorable. And not just for me, but for everyone who attends a LIVE show.

Seth Shomes, my incredible agent. Thank you for working so hard each day. Because of you, I will be touring nationally and internationally for years to come!

Sherry Ferdinandi, my CFO and business manager, your expertise allows me to focus on my passion while you expertly handle the business end. Your advocacy for my best interests does not go unnoticed.

Alice and Patrick, the creative minds behind my marketing, your ability to transform ideas into visual masterpieces is nothing short of miraculous.

James Melia, my editor: Thank you for working so closely with me on this new book! Your can-do attitude is what I needed to keep moving forward!

Jeremie Ruby-Strauss, thank you for giving me the opportunity to publish my very first book with Simon & Schuster. It's because of you I am now on my third!

Frances Yackel, thank you for being such a great project manager, thank you for keeping track of everything and for the constant communication you have kept going with the team to get this book to the finish line.

Caroline Pallotta, your dedication to keeping the book's timeline on track, though often behind the scenes, has been crucial to our timely success.

Sarah Wright, the eagle-eyed proofreader, your skills have saved me from numerous grammatical errors, and thank you for keeping my writing polished and professional.

Jennifer Robinson, my literary publicist, I am so thankful to have you! Thank you for the book tour, the celebrity introductions, and all you have made happen!

Mackenzie Hickey, my marketing specialist, your efforts to ensure my book's presence in bookstores is a dream come true every time I see it on display.

John Vairo and Lisa Litwack, my artistic visionaries, the book cover is a testament to your creative genius. I love the way you have brought my vision to life on the cover!

Jen Bergstrom, thank you for helping spread this book's message of comfort to those in grief around the globe.

Aimee Bell, for your support and behind-the-scenes magic, I eagerly anticipate the readers' reactions to our collective work.

Jen Long, your enthusiasm from our first meeting at Simon & Schuster has been a source of joy and inspiration.

Sally Marvin, for your expertise in publicity and marketing, I am immensely thankful.

To my friends, family, and everyone at Simon & Schuster: I am blessed beyond words to have such a supportive and talented team by my side.